MY LIFE WITH THE ROYAL BALLET
AS A DANCER AND TEACHER

1953. The author, photographed by Maurice Seymour in New York.

MY LIFE WITH THE ROYAL BALLET
AS A DANCER AND TEACHER

Valerie Adams

Noverre Press

This book is dedicated to my dear mother Eileen, without whom none of this would have been possible.

and

In gratitude to 'Madam' for forming the Teachers' Course in 1964 and inviting me to be at her side.

First published in 2014 by The Noverre Press,
Southwold House, Isington Road, Binsted, Hampshire, GU34 4PH

© Valerie Adams 2014
ISBN: 978-1-906830-66-3

A CIP catalogue for this title is available from the British Library

Printed in Great Britain

Contents

Illustrations

(between pages 70 and 71)

Introduction

In 1943 the seed was sown for my unique and rewarding career with the Sadler's Wells Ballet, now known as The Royal Ballet, both as a member of the company at the Royal Opera House, Covent Garden, London, and as a full-time ballet teacher at The Royal Ballet School.

After leaving the company I had the privilege of being trained to teach by Ninette de Valois, founder of The Royal Ballet, always known as 'Madam'. After six months I was made a junior member of the full-time ballet staff.

In 1956 I was invited by the Dutch Government to form a Ballet School at the Koninklijk Conservatorium voor Muziek at The Hague, Holland, to be run on the same lines as the Sadler's Wells School in London. My brief was to prepare dancers for the three Dutch ballet companies. Madam said to me 'go and get on with it dear, it will be good for you'.

By 1961 the Ballet School was well established and running smoothly with students graduating into the companies each year. I felt it was now time for me to return to London. However, it was not quite so straightforward and I needed to stay until Christmas of that year. Happily, by April 1962, I was back on the full-time ballet staff at The Royal Ballet School

One day in 1963 Madam invited me to lunch. I must say my first thoughts were 'what have I done wrong?' but I soon came to my senses and realised it must be for some other reason. After getting out of the Tube at Hammersmith, to my amazement, she was suddenly running across the busy roads in order to catch the bus, with me following behind her as fast as I could. After arriving at her home and sitting me down, she said, 'I am thinking of starting a teachers' course. Would you like to be at my side? Are you interested?' What an honour! Naturally my answer was, 'Yes please.' The Craftsman's Course as it was first called, opened in September 1964, and my position was general assistant to the course.

For the next eight years, we worked together, Madam still passing on her valuable knowledge to me, and in 1971 she made me the course director. From then on my life was totally dedicated to running the course. There are 324 graduates all around the world as ambassadors for The Royal Ballet School. Madam once said to me, 'I wonder if the time will ever come when one of them will be teaching for us in the school.' Well, that did happen many years ago. There are a number still teaching there today, and it is such a joy for me to see them. Much more will be said about the course later.

As it turned out it was fifty years from the first time I went to have classes with Madam in 1950 at Barons Court, until I taught my last class there in 2000.

This is the story of my life. However, it would not be complete without first mentioning my parents' families, so that is where the story and adventure begins.

Chapter 1

About the family

My grandfather, Henry John Adams, was born in 1870 in Pembroke Dock, Wales, and came from a family of mariners. In 1884 he signed on as an apprentice to his father in the art of shipwrighting for seven years. Later he was commissioned to the rank of carpenter and then shipwright officer in the early Royal Australian Navy, and served in the First World War in numerous ships of the Australian Fleet. Being a carpenter, he had made his own sea chest, and over the years it has been very useful for things like blankets and pillows. I still have it to this day.

My father's mother, Elizabeth, was born in 1885 to Mary and Andrew Agnew. She was one of seven children, three boys and four girls, and they lived in Newry, County Down, Northern Ireland.

In 1904 when Elizabeth was 19, Andrew moved all his family to Simonstown in South Africa and opened a canning factory. While there, Elizabeth became headmistress of a girls college and it was during the next few years that she met her future husband, my grandfather, whose ship was in dock at the naval base at Simonstown. Sometime later they married and returned to England, making their home in Portsmouth, where he was based with the Royal Navy.

My father, Robert Henry Agnew Adams, always called Bob, was born in 1910. About two years later, my grandfather was lent to the Royal Australian Navy, so that meant a move for the family to New South Wales. Their home was at Hunters Hill, and he received his education at Malvern School, Sydney, all his spare time being spent sailing a boat on Sydney harbour. At the age of 16 years he was apprenticed to the Commonwealth and Dominion Line trading between England and Australia.

In 1930 the family returned to this country, and as my grandfather was now retired, they decided to move to Bournemouth, Hampshire, now Dorset. A house was purchased in Harewood Avenue off Pokesdown Hill, not far from Kings Park. At that time there were still fields nearby. This house was a good size and up to date, situated on a hill, with crazy paving steps to the front door. As a child I was to fall down these on a number of occasions.

My father had wanted to go to Dartmouth Royal Naval College but was just too old when they returned to this country, so he joined the Royal Naval Reserve as a midshipman and sub-lieutenant, serving in HM Ships.

It was through a mutual friend who lived opposite that my parents met and became good friends. They both enjoyed ballroom dancing and Bob would take Eileen to tea dances at the Lucullus Room in the Pavilion Theatre. I understand they made a very good couple and won a number of competitions.

In 1933 many ships were laid up due to the shipping depression and my father transferred from the R.N.R. to the R.N.V.S.R. A friend persuaded him to leave the sea and take a shore job, especially as he had become engaged to my mother, so he joined F.W. Woolworth & Co Ltd. as assistant manager, first of all in the Boscombe Branch. They married in 1934 and were living in a flat in the Winton area when I was born the following year. Not too long afterwards, my father was sent to the branch in Worthing, Sussex, and we lived there in a flat for some months before he was sent to the main Bournemouth branch. It was at this time that we moved into the house at Harewood Avenue with my grandparents. I was then about three years old. These few years were to prove that working indoors and away from the sea really did not suit my father, so when war was declared in September 1939, he was happy to be immediately called up in the R.N.V.R. He served as Captain of Convoy Escort Vessels, Trawlers and Corvettes in the Atlantic and Mediterranean, and in 1942 he was mentioned in despatches for Distinguished Service in the North Russian convoys.

More will come out later about my grandparents and this house, as it was to become our home for a number of years prior to moving to London.

* * *

My mother's father, Albert James Thacker Foster, and her mother, Rose Eliza Baker were married in Faversham, Kent, on the 20th August 1900. Bert, 23 years old, an insurance agent and Rose, twenty, decided to leave Kent and also move to Bournemouth. They chose to set up home in the Southbourne area, within walking distance of the sea. They lived in several places before moving into a newly-built house in West Road, which was to be their home for the rest of their lives.

Their first two children were boys, Reginald and Beresford, always known as Reg and Berry. The next two children died as infants, and then my mother Eileen came along, the only girl. Reg was twelve years older than she, but they got on very well together and later, when she was going to her first party, he taught her to dance.

Rose apparently was not very strong and spent a lot of time in hospital during my mother's childhood. She was a very good needlewoman and made most of her own clothes and those for my mother, until she too was able to make her own. Rose also did crochet work, collars for dresses, borders for table cloths and napkins, and very small edgings and designs for handkerchiefs.

They were a very musical family. Reg and Berry played the violin, Rose and Eileen played the piano and Berry sang with Eileen. This was something they could all share.

Bert was a mathematician, I think that must have been the reason why my mother enjoyed working with figures. He was the one who was a big influence in her life and would take her out to places, for example, fishing at Christchurch Harbour. She always said she learnt so much from him.

Eileen went to the Bournemouth School for Girls. When she was leaving, she was offered a scholarship to study singing, but unfortunately she could not take up the place because her parents were unable to afford the accommodation. She then joined the staff of the new branch of Boots in Bournemouth. They soon discovered her artistic talent and made her a window dresser, which she thoroughly enjoyed.

When my parents wanted to get married, Rose was not happy about this at all. She felt that my mother should stay at home and look after her. She was not an invalid, and at that time was in better health than she had been for a long while. However, when it came to the wedding in 1934, Bert was there to give my mother away but Rose did not attend.

When World War II started, Reg joined the Air force and later married Madge. Berry joined the Army and married Flo. Unfortunately he did not live very long after that, and because neither of them had children, I was the only grandchild.

Chapter 2

Wartime travels

My earliest memory is that of my father coming home with his naval uniform, having been called up for World War II as soon as war was declared in 1939, and my mother saying 'do go upstairs and put it on, so that I can take some photographs'. We went out into the garden and my mother took them with the Brownie box camera. Soon after, we were issued with gas masks. Whenever we went out, these had to be taken with us. Also, we had to wear some form of identification, mine being a bracelet with my identity number engraved on it.

After war was declared, a tremendous amount of work was done to defend our country in case of invasion. All beaches around the south coast had rolls of barbed wire along them. There was no way one could go down to the beach, and it was not until some time after the war that all this was removed, and one could once again walk by the water's edge and go into the sea.

In the dining room, a large Morrison shelter was erected. It seemed to take up at least half the space. It was near the inner wall and I could just squeeze in behind when we used it as a table. The two armchairs were placed either side of the fireplace and it was there that my grandmother used to sit to do her knitting. She was making socks for servicemen – that was her part towards the war effort. At night we had to put shutters up against the windows so that not a speck of light could be seen from outside. The air raid wardens going round would always knock on the door if they could see any light.

In January 1940 rationing was introduced and we each had a book with coupons in it. It was amazing to see the small amount one was allowed to have and how inventive one had to be to make it go round. I shall never forget the dried eggs and the Nestlé's condensed milk. There was no Cadbury chocolate or biscuits for a long time, and even when they did return, they had to be ordered. I always remember going to the grocer's shop and six chocolate biscuits being weighed out in a piece of newspaper.

My grandparents were using the front double bedroom and I had the single one looking out over St Catherine's Hill, a lovely view because we were high up. In there I had the sea chest I spoke of earlier. It was a very good place for my toys to sit. My parents had the back bedroom overlooking the garden. My father, who was stationed around the south coast at the beginning of the war, was able to have a day or so on leave, and when he arrived, he would throw up some gravel against my mother's bedroom window. Then she knew it was he, always a time for rejoicing, and put the kettle on. He was never able to let us know when he was coming home.

At the early stage of the war my father was based at Portland Bill, Weymouth, and as he was expecting to be there for a while, he suggested to my mother that she stay at the Wyke Regis Hotel for a few days, which she did, and then decided to return to Bournemouth to fetch me. When we returned to the hotel the next day, we discovered that my father had had to call out the marines the night before, as there was a suspected invasion around the south coast. The whole place was swarming with troops, all lying on the floor trying to get some sleep. We made our way to my mother's room and it too was occupied with troops. When my mother said she was staying there, the officer in charge just said 'Sorry madam, you will have to find a place elsewhere.' Another naval officer's wife offered to put us up for a few days, until it was possible to return home. They had a lovely garden and I was able to play with her daughter, whose cat seemed quite happy to be pushed around in her doll's pram.

* * *

It was not too long before we were off on our next adventure in Belfast, Northern Ireland. The intention was obviously to stay some time because all our furniture at Harewood Avenue was put into store. My father was being sent to join another ship off the Irish coast, and we were to travel with him on a troop ship.

What a nightmare! The train journey from Bournemouth to Stranraer in Scotland seemed so long. Fortunately, I had my little case with me which contained a Bible, my koala bear and knitting. My grandmother had taught me, and I was knitting my father a naval scarf – this kept me well occupied, and I enjoyed seeing it grow. Then on to the troopship. My mother and I seemed to be the only civilian passengers, and my father said 'If anyone tries to stop you, just say that you are travelling with me and that all your luggage is already in the hold.' It was a very rough crossing, and besides the troops, the ship was also carrying a herd of cows, all very tightly packed in the front of the ship and making such a noise. Eventually we arrived at the port of Larne in Northern Ireland and then on to a hotel in Belfast, my father, of course, leaving us to go and report to his ship. While there, we were invited by some relatives to visit their home. It was winter time and I stepped onto a frozen pond and fell through. My mother was not best pleased. I was wearing a new kilt and I can still remember her washing it out in the basin of our hotel bedroom.

Soon a ground floor flat was found in Belfast. All I can remember about it was the very large kitchen with a stone floor, and on one wall, a pulley to dry clothes.

After some time of not seeing my father, he came home with all his oiled wool jumpers, sea boot stockings, and balaclavas, and said he would be returning the next day for some leave and during that time he would wash all these things. He told my mother not to attempt to do it, because it would be far too heavy for her to lift when wet, (no washing machines around then). Of course it was no good saying anything like that to my mother. As soon as he had left, she said, 'let's do it all before Daddy comes home and then we will have more time to spend with him'. I was no use to her – I could only just see over the sink. However, she managed to do it and had it all hanging up dripping on the stone floor. That evening we had a phone call from my father, saying 'be prepared for a shock, we are off to Glasgow, Scotland, tomorrow'. My mother just looked at all that wet washing, reached for the kit bags, and together we stuffed it all inside. There was really nothing else she could do.

The date was the 29th August 1940, and we had a problem, because we had entered Ireland on my father's passport and we had no passports to leave. We therefore spent all night having photographs taken and arranging for exit permits. Of course, there was all the packing up to do. My father arrived in the morning to help with that, and then we were off on the next adventure.

* * *

I have no recollection of being on a ship again or the train journey to Glasgow, I suppose being up all the night before had made me sleep through everything. However, on arrival at Glasgow I was wide awake, because there had been an air raid the night before and broken glass was everywhere in the station. My father said that he must leave us to go to the ship, and pointing to an information bureau, told us that they should be able to suggest somewhere for us to stay. I cannot imagine what must have been going through my mother's head at that moment, she just seemed to take everything in her stride. We had actually arrived during the first air raids on Glasgow. We were given the address of a place to stay that night, and I know we moved several times before ending up in a cottage in Gourock overlooking the Clyde, watching the ships going out and returning. We did not hear anything from my father for three weeks, and as the raids were going on every night, he did not know if we were alive and vice versa. When eventually, he found us and had a few days leave, he was absolutely exhausted, because he never did get the leave that was due to him when in Ireland.

One night, he woke up and asked what the noise was. My mother just said it was another raid going on. 'Why are you not up,' he replied and she just said there was nowhere to go, there were no shelters around.

On one occasion we saw my father's ship go past and then return later. It had gone over a mine and had to return to port for repairs. How any ships got through I will never know because we only had to look outside the front door to see the bombs dropping further down the road at the mouth of the Clyde.

My father soon realised how bad the situation was becoming all round the country and said that my mother and I must return to Bournemouth; and anyway it was time for me to go to school.

* * *

It was lovely to be back at Harewood Avenue. Our furniture came out of store and once again I was reunited with my toys, which had been put in the bottom drawer of my mother's dressing table, and in the garage was my blue painted tricycle. Also, there were all my small gardening tools, and I could be gardening again, which I enjoyed so much. I was soon enrolled at the local kindergarten school just a few minutes walk away and stayed there until I was nine years old. Sometimes, if they were short of a teacher for maths, they would call on my mother to help.

My mother was called upon to be a fire watch warden and had to learn how to put out incendiaries, small bombs which caused fires. She made us laugh when she told us about her training – having to put on men's dungarees and crawl across the ground to put out the fires. As soon as the air raid siren went off, she was out of the house, leaving me with my grandmother and our neighbour, who would come in through a gate in the fence, so she could be with us in the Morrison shelter. My mother had to check all the people living alone in the road and was there if anyone needed help. She would be out until the All Clear sounded. Of course when it was in the night, she was out in total darkness with only a torch with the light mainly covered over. When we went to bed, we always had a set of clothes on a chair ready to be picked up the moment the siren went off. It could be several times during the night.

The garage by now was full of coal, divided into three sections, from floor to ceiling; one for anthracite for the kitchen stove which heated the water, one for coke, and the other for ordinary coal. Coal fires were the only form of heating in the house. The coal used to be delivered by a horse and cart, and the coal man would wear a leather cap and leather piece across his shoulders and lift the bag onto his back. It was hard work carrying it up the steep slope to the garage. The horse was so patient having to stop and wait outside each house, I would often go out and talk to it.

In September 1940 the Blitz over London started, and that really began to make a difference – the Spitfires having dog fights with enemy aircraft overhead and the shrapnel falling on the asbestos garage roof. If the Germans had any bombs left over, they would drop them over Bournemouth before flying back over the sea.

While all this was going on, my grandfather became unwell and he passed on in 1942.

Also that year, my father came home on leave after being on the convoys to Russia. We were so excited because we had not seen or heard from him for many months, and we went to Pokesdown Station to meet him. For a while, we wondered if he had missed the train. You see, he now had a full beard, but we did not know that and it made him look so different. It was only when he walked towards us that we really knew it was he. I think it took time for my mother to get over the shock, and I know she asked him to remove it. Those Russian convoys had made it necessary because of the cold – my father said they were a terrible experience for all involved.

Chapter 3

Early days dancing

After returning to Bournemouth, I used to play with the bank manager's son, Michael Arthur, who lived on Pokesdown Hill nearby. Like myself he was eight years old, and had the most beautiful dappled grey rocking horse which I enjoyed riding while he played with his trains.

One day his sister Mary, who was twelve, came into the room and asked if I would like to go to dancing class with her the next Saturday. I remember jumping off the horse and running all the way home to ask my mother if I could go. She said that Saturday was not convenient. However, I could go the following week on condition that she did not have anything to do with it.

Little did she know, when she said that, how much she was going to be needed in so many different ways, and how it would totally affect her life.

The Wessex School of Dancing was situated in the corner of the Royal Arcade at Boscombe, an excellent position, and it was there that I received all my training up to the age of sixteen. The school had three studios with changing rooms, plus a room for keeping costumes. It was run by two very gifted teachers, who had just taken over the school prior to my going there.

Ida Stewart taught all the Royal Academy of Dancing (now the Royal Academy of Dance) Children's Five Grade examinations, together with Greek dancing, having studied with Ruby Ginner. Later she became an examiner. She also taught National Folk Dance and Spanish dancing, having studied with Elsa Brunelleschi. Besides all this she taught ballroom dancing at the school in the evenings. Ida was truly one of those very rare, gifted teachers of children, and I was so fortunate to have been one of her pupils.

Elizabeth Collins (always known as Betty) taught the Royal Academy Major Syllabus from Elementary to Solo Seal. She also taught Tap, Modern and Musical Comedy. She was very musical and had a gift for choreography, always being able to bring out the best from her students.

Both of them taught dancing at various schools all around Bournemouth and Swanage during the daytime and were always keen to keep learning and be up to date with what was going on. Betty attended all the two weeks summer courses which Ninette de Valois gave to teachers, starting in 1947. They made a good team, and to have been able to produce at least six dancers for The Royal Ballet Companies was a tremendous achievement.

After going to classes on Saturday mornings for a few months, Ida called me over one week, saying that she would like to enter me for the forthcoming Musical Festival and needed to speak to my mother about it? 'Oh no', I said, 'she does not want to have anything to do with my dancing.' Ida just gently replied, 'do ask her if she could come and see me'. Well, that took some persuading on my part, after what my mother had said, but happily she did agree to my entering and ensured that I had a little blue tunic and that my hair was neatly tied back for the occasion.

The outcome of that first Musical Festival, held at St. Peters Hall, was that the adjudicator awarded me second place in the Ballet Class 9 – 12 years, and said that if I had done more difficult steps she would have given me first place. I had only been dancing about six months and had my ninth birthday the previous week. Because of this result, my mother felt that perhaps she needed to become a little more involved and help me to remember things.

Soon afterwards, I was entered for Grade 1, and these examinations were held in the basement studio. It was nice being in familiar surroundings and having our wonderful pianist, Miss Dally. This examination was followed by the other four grades, one every six months.

In September of that year, 1944, I moved to Dean House School, a small school run by Mrs Evans in her house, and she was very strict. The only help she had was one other teacher. It was about twenty minutes walk from our home, and I was there between the ages of nine and 12.

Because of the war and clothing coupons, there was no school uniform as such, so we had to wear a brown overall over our clothes. My mother had been given the pattern and told where she could purchase the material, and then she made it up.

The advantage of this school was that Ida taught dancing to the pupils there, once a week in the local church hall, so together with my one at the studio I was now having two classes per week.

Soon after the war ended in 1945, and the Morrison shelter had been removed from the dining room, my grandmother was asked by some friends if she could look after their upright piano for a time, as they were moving and did not want to put it into store. My mother thought this was a good opportunity for me to have some piano lessons. Although I wanted to be able to play, it seemed an uphill battle. I did take a couple of grade exams before the piano had to be returned, but kept on with the theory and took several of the higher grades.

By the spring of 1946 I had passed all my five RAD Grades, and moved up to the Elementary class taught by Betty. My mother thought that I would benefit from having a private lesson in addition to my weekly class because I seemed to be having such difficulty in remembering the steps. She also said she would sit in the corner out of everyone's way and make notes of the corrections given, so that we could go over them before the next lesson. She never pushed me, but was there to give encouraging support. She always said, 'if you really understand the reason why and how, you will do it so much better'. Betty was quite happy with this arrangement, as she could see how much it was helping me.

My father was not demobbed until much later. However, he did have some leave in the summer of 1946 and we went on our first holiday together to Teignmouth in Devon. I took my practice clothes and ballet shoes with me, just in case I should need them.

We arrived at the small hotel in the late afternoon, and as we were exploring the rooms, I suddenly heard the RAD Elementary music being played. The sound was coming from a room at the back of the hotel. After making some enquiries, we discovered that a local dancing teacher, Miss Spencer-Edwards, hired the room to give classes. I then asked my mother if I could have a lesson from her. So after the class had finished we spoke to her and she agreed. What a blessing I had my practice clothes with me. After that I don't think I ever went away without them.

When the lesson was over, Miss Spencer-Edwards said it would be good for me if I could have a lesson from Miss Sybil Spencer, an RAD Examiner who lived at Newton Abbott some miles away. This was all arranged. We had a long bus ride through the countryside to reach her studio but this proved to be very worthwhile. She was an excellent teacher, and years later when I was a teacher we became good friends.

* * *

1947 was a very exciting year in which my life seemed to go forward by leaps and bounds. In February I took my RAD Elementary examination and had to wear a tutu for the first time. As there was no net available, it was made from paint straining muslin. The exam was held in the Norman and Saxon ballet studio, over the Fifty Shillings Men's Tailors shop in the centre of Bournemouth, and the examiner was Phyllis Bedells.

I was happy with the exam result. However, my mother said that we needed to have a serious talk, because passing that exam made me a member of the RAD, and that meant she would need to pay a subscription each year of one guinea. Was I really serious about wanting to go on with my dancing, because that was a lot of money to pay out. I begged her to allow me to continue and she just said that we would need to take one step at a time.

Later, on the 18th of February, Betty was going to London to see the Sadler's Wells Ballet Company performing *Swan Lake* at the Royal Opera House, and invited my mother and me to accompany her. What a thrill, our first visit to London! Betty particularly wanted to see Wendy Winn, a former pupil of the Wessex School who was now a member of the corps de ballet. That performance was a wonderful inspiration to me and from then on I had a goal to be able to join the Sadler's Wells Ballet Company.

After the performance we went round to the stage door and asked to see Wendy. While we were talking to her, Ninette de Valois came by and asked Wendy how her mother was getting on, as she had been seriously ill. Wendy said she was much better and that she was going to see her that weekend. Madam immediately said, 'do you have enough money for the fare?' That statement made a tremendous impression on me and was one I shall never forget, because it showed the loving, caring side to Madam which in later years I was to experience on a number of occasions.

Another exciting thing that year was the beginning of the Bournemouth Ballet Club, which was formed by Madame Murilova,

Elizabeth Collins, Ida Stewart and Alice Woodward, the four leading dance teachers in the area.

The aim of the club was to increase the appreciation and knowledge of the art of ballet and to give young people from a variety of different schools and traditions the opportunity to meet, dance and give performances together. These aims were achieved by inviting well known lecturers, teachers and dancers to visit the club, and to include everyone, whether they were dancing or watching, for their greater interest and understanding.

My mother and I were founder members. There were twenty-one of us at the first meeting on Sunday, 20th April in Madame Murilova's studio in the centre of Bournemouth, and the first lecturer was Joan Lawson.

Later on in September, Phyllis Bedells gave the senior students a class, followed by questions and answers about her remarkable career.

The number of members joining grew very quickly (it seemed to be the only thing happening on Sunday afternoons) and it soon became necessary to move to the Municipal College Hall at the Lansdowne. Meetings took place once a month and the classes were very popular. A junior class would be given before tea, and it was during this break, that the guests were asked to sign a large tablecloth, after which a lady from the club would stitch it over by hand in a different colour. This ritual was then followed by a senior class. There could be up to forty students in a class and an audience of parents and teachers all sitting round the sides watching. These classes were such a treat. I remember being taught by all the teachers from the Sadler's Wells School. The first performance was given in 1950 at St Peter's Hall and the choreography was arranged by Elizabeth Collins.

Ninette de Valois became president of the club in 1950 and she too gave classes and lectures. Years later when I was teaching at The Royal Ballet School, I deputised for her on several occasions as well as being invited there myself.

In 1992, Barbara Fewster took over the Presidency to celebrate the club's forty-five years of continuous existence. Sadly, in May 2010 after 63 years and as the longest running ballet club in the country, it had to close, due to lack of interest (too many things now going on during Sundays). All the memorabilia about the club, including the two tablecloths with all those autographs of famous names, are now being cared for in The Royal Ballet School archives, at White Lodge in Richmond Park.

* * *

For the Musical Festival in 1947, I was entered in the Classes for Ballet, Demi-Caractère, and National. To be accurate for the National costumes, my mother and I would go to the library, where she would trace a picture on greaseproof paper of the costume I was to wear and make notes of the correct colours. She always wanted the details to be accurate and this was often commented on by the adjudicator.

This particular year I had to be entered in the Classes 12–15 years, and as I had just turned twelve the week before, my parents said jokingly that they would give me a watch if by any chance I came first in the ballet class. Looking at the other candidates, I felt I did not have a hope, and also the adjudicator was Noreen Bush who we knew was very tough and hard to please. However, to my surprise she called my number for first place. I always said I could hear that watch ticking as I stood on the stage. Years later, when talking to Noreen Bush I told her it was all because of her marking, that I received my first watch.

Continuing on with this exciting year, we had another trip to London in June, to see Wendy in *The Three-Cornered Hat*, one of the ballets in the triple bill that night. It was always so thrilling to see the company and to be able to go backstage afterwards was amazing. Each time we went I used to get Wendy to sign my autograph book, so that is why I have a record of our visits.

When only staying for a night, we always tried to fit in as much as possible and this time I was able to attend an open class with Vera Volkova at the famous dance studios in West Street. What an experience at the age of twelve, to be in the same class as ballerinas and soloists from the company! It was lovely to watch Beryl Grey, who was there that day. It was not a question of thinking 'I am not able to do those steps' – I just had to follow and do the best I could and try to take on board as many corrections as possible. Over the coming years, I was grateful to attend a few more times. It was such a privilege to be able to go to these classes and it certainly gave me inspiration to work as hard as I possibly could.

In July, when I finished at Dean House School, Mrs Evans, the headmistress, gave me a ballet book for making good progress, entitled *Sadler's Wells Ballet at Covent Garden*. The pictures were all black and white, but that did not matter. I loved looking at them and dreaming that perhaps one day I might be there too.

* * *

In September, I started at St Mary's Gate. This school was chosen because Betty and Ida taught dancing there, although I would not be attending their classes. The headmistress was very understanding when she heard that I needed to be able to have more dance classes in the week and kindly agreed that I could have two afternoons off, instead of playing games. The rest of my form were not pleased – why could they not have time to go riding etc.? However, it was just one of those things one had to deal with.

The school was situated quite near to the sea on the cliffs at Southbourne, and when the wind was blowing there was plenty of sand in all the wrong places. It seemed to get in through the sash windows. The classroom was very cold and in the winter I used to sit by the one bar electric fire. My grandmother knitted me some knee warmers and mittens for my hands to try and help me keep warm. In the summer, I would sit by the window, a wonderful view overlooking the bay, with Swanage to the right and the Isle of Wight to the left, something never to be forgotten. I had been given a bicycle the year before and this now proved to be very useful, as there was no direct bus route, and I was able to ride my bike to school.

At the studio, I was now learning Greek dancing, which was helping me to relax and be less tense, and to develop more flow of movement. All this was an advantage to my ballet as well.

In February 1948 I took my RAD Intermediate and fortunately was successful.

The Wessex School was now being asked to give displays at hotels for after dinner entertainment, and at garden parties in the summer. This was all very good experience. The school was also preparing for a full length performance at the Hippodrome Theatre.

Various costumes were now required and my mother was always asking friends if they had any spare material or sheets that could be dyed to make costumes. I can still remember seeing a tutu hanging on the line to dry, which she had dyed for a tiger lily costume, and it coming out all shades of yellow – just what she wanted. There was another time that always made us laugh, when I had to have a headdress, for a solo from *Swan Lake*. My mother needed some white feathers to make it and the only person she could think of to ask was the fishmonger, who also sold poultry. After a few days, he produced a bag of white feathers. My mother then set to and made it, sticking all the feathers individually onto a base. As usual she made an excellent job of it.

Tights were also a problem. We wore black woollen ones for practice in the winter and pink cotton at other times. They were really awful, because when one knelt down and then stood up, they were all baggy at the knees. Later, my mother was able to purchase some pure silk opera hose from Burnetts in London, which she sewed onto briefs.

My hair was very straight and needed to be curled, so my mother used curling tongs and put them in the gas ring to heat. How she knew how long to leave them, I will never know, but she never singed my hair and it seemed to do the trick, although it was a tedious operation.

I think the bus conductors got used to us travelling around with two large brown suitcases and often there were props as well. Among the many which caused comments, were a birdcage, a large hoop and a picture frame which I could stand in. Fortunately this came apart for travelling.

In December of that year, I took my first Greek dancing examination, which was Grade 4, and a year later took Grade 5.

* * *

The next year and a half was taken up mainly with studying for my RAD Advanced. This was a very difficult time for me. I seemed to have outgrown my strength and was all arms and legs, and I was finding the technique required more than difficult. My mother felt it might help if I could have a private lesson from one of the London teachers. This was arranged with Phyllis Bedells, in April 1949. She was very kind and helpful and encouraged me to keep working. I think hearing a different voice giving me corrections did help.

On this visit, we were also able to arrange to see another ballet performance at the Royal Opera House and saw Wendy performing in *Don Juan* and *Apparitions*. To be at any performance was such a thrill to me, because it was very seldom that we saw any ballet performances in Bournemouth.

I took the RAD Advanced exam in November of that year and was very grateful to pass it. There was now just one more examination I could take, the highest award of the Royal Academy which was the Solo Seal, but one had to be fifteen to take it. If I entered for it in the session held in March 1951, I would have fifteen months to prepare for it. Betty had not previously entered anyone for this exam, so it was a learning experience for both of us.

* * *

In January 1950 we were in London again just for one night and I was able to go to another open class in West Street with Vera Volkova, always an amazing experience. One never knew who might be attending from the company, and to be in the same class – words cannot really describe one's feelings. In the evening we went to see the ballet *Cinderella* at the Royal Opera House. Going to these performances was so wonderful, and every time it encouraged me to stick to my goal: to be able to join the company.

By the following April, my mother thought that perhaps it was time for me to have another private lesson in London. I think she could see, that because Betty was my only teacher and I was the most advanced student in my class, I needed to hear another voice and be seen through the eyes of someone else. This time we decided on Noreen Bush, who we knew was very tough and strong on technique. I must admit she scared me, but I knew she was only trying to help and I was grateful for her advice.

During this trip, we went to Freed's, the ballet shoemakers in St Martins Lane and it was then that I had my introduction to the famous indomitable Mrs Freed. She was, from then on, the one who would fit my pointe shoes and find a maker in the firm who would make shoes to suit my feet.

As we were in London, we could not miss the opportunity to go to the ballet that night and saw *Scènes de Ballet* and *Les Patineurs*. Of course we later went backstage to see Wendy, who always gave us such a welcome.

In the summer of 1950 another friend from the Wessex School went to London and joined the Sadler's Wells Company at Covent Garden. Catherine Boulton was a year or so older than myself and had been at boarding school, so our paths had only crossed occasionally – usually during the summer holidays when we were performing together.

My mother and I were now looking to the future and I was longing to move towards my goal. If I wished to go to London the next year, then I needed to be dancing every day. So the decision was made to leave school at the end of July and have a tutor. A very pleasant lady was found, who was happy to arrange a programme of lessons around my dancing timetable. I was then able to join up with the other full-time students at the Wessex, and this enabled me to learn other things, including Mime and Spanish Dancing.

In September of that year Madam started to give classes to advanced students of teachers who had attended her two weeks summer courses, and Betty had done these. The classes were held at the Sadler's Wells School at Barons Court on Friday afternoons 4.30p.m. – 5.30p.m. I was able to attend, not every week, but whenever it was possible. Betty would take me up to London and I would try and do some homework during the train journeys. Betty was able to watch, so that was good, because she could then help me afterwards with the things I was finding difficult. These classes were a new experience for me, because it was the first time that I was in a class with students of my own standard. It was good to have the competition and be able to watch the others and try to do better. On our way back to Waterloo for the 6.30p.m. train, we often met Madam going home, and Betty would have the opportunity to talk to her about the Ballet Club, of which she was now the President.

The Solo Seal examination was looming fast. It consisted of doing a classical class, which included certain requirements, followed by a classical solo which was printed in the RAD Gazette, and which Betty could learn at their forthcoming special week, and a *demi-caractère* solo selected by the candidate.

After learning the classical solo, it proved to be more than a challenge, because somehow I could not get through it from beginning to end without stopping. As much as I tried and practised, it still proved to be a problem.

My mother had the idea that perhaps it was time for another

private lesson, as nearly a year had passed since the last one. So we decided on Marion Knight, who had choreographed the solo. She was as helpful as she could, but said that I did not have the stamina to get through the solo, and that I should not expect to pass. That was not very encouraging, but I knew this was my last opportunity to try for it, if I was planning to go to London later that year, and decided to do my best and have a go.

The time for the Solo Seal exam arrived. We had to go to London the day before, to the Royal Academy in Holland Park Avenue, where the candidates were allowed fifteen minutes in the studio, to run through their solos. Miss Dally, our pianist, was there too, to play for my solos. What a wonderful support she always was and completely reliable. Betty was there to help me place the floor patterns correctly in the different shaped studio that I was unfamiliar with. However, there was still the problem of completing the classical solo. I could see Betty standing there in the corner with tears running down her face. All I could say to her was that I could only do my best. That evening we all went to the Royal Opera House, to see Margot Fonteyn in *The Sleeping Beauty*. If that could not give me the inspiration needed, I don't know what could. It was a truly wonderful performance.

At the RAD the next day there were three candidates and I was number three. The examiners were Dame Adeline Genée, Tamara Karsavina, and Phyllis Bedells. Ruth French was taking the class. What a line up, all having been famous ballerinas in their time. I completed everything that I needed to do in the class, and then it was the solos. I went back to the changing room to put on my tutu and asked my mother to stay positive and to know that if it was right, I would be able to complete the solo. Inspired by that performance the night before, I was able to do so, and happily returned to the changing room with the good news. On to the *demi-caractère* solo, which I always enjoyed dancing. Betty was naturally relieved to hear that all had gone well.

The exam over, and as it was a Friday, I asked if we could go over to the Sadler's Wells School, for me to attend the class with Madam. I changed into my practice clothes and we found a taxi to take us. I had been the week before and mentioned that I hoped to make it in time, so Madam was not surprised when I entered the studio just as she was starting. After the class, we were back to Waterloo Station for the 6.30p.m train home. What a trip to London that had been –

one I shall never forget.

Two weeks later, a letter arrived, informing me that I had been awarded the Solo Seal. I was the first person from Bournemouth to receive it.

The next part of the plan was to audition for the Sadler's Wells Theatre Ballet. I felt that perhaps because it was the smaller of the two companies, it might give me more opportunities. My audition was held on stage at the theatre in front of the director, Ursula Moreton. After it was over, she said she was very sorry that she could not accept me, because that week she had received a message from Madam that she was not to accept anyone straight into the company. From now on, it would be necessary to go to the school first.

My next move was to apply for an audition to go to the Sadler's Wells School. That was to take place a few weeks later, which meant another trip to London. This time, I was dancing in front of Madam and Ailne Phillips, the principal, and Winifred Edwards took the audition. After waiting a few weeks, I heard that I had been accepted.

It was now a very busy time at the Wessex School, because we were preparing for the Musical Festival the first week in June. This was to be my last one, and I was entered for Ballet, *Demi-Caractère*, National, Greek, and Musical Comedy.

One day, when I was having a private ballet lesson, the pianist in the arcade outside the studio started to play 'We'll Gather Lilacs', the famous Ivor Novello tune from *Perchance To Dream*. Betty stopped my lesson and said she had always wanted to choreograph a musical comedy solo for me to that music. She then asked Miss Dally, who was playing for me at the time, to go down the arcade and buy the sheet music. It was actually our family's favourite tune, and my mother immediately started to sketch a design for the dress, in two shades of lilac. When Miss Dally returned, Betty immediately set to and choreographed the whole solo at one go. She was totally inspired and I had great difficulty in keeping up with her flow of thoughts, but it all came together so beautifully.

As the Festival drew near, we heard that my father was coming home on leave and would be able to watch me dance for the first time. So that was something special! When it came to the day, I was grateful to do well in all the classes, and the Musical Comedy was the last. It was a very large class of thirty or more, but somehow, when I started to dance, everything seemed to go so quiet, and it was wonderful to be at one with the music. The audience started to applaud well before the end, a very special moment in time. It was therefore not surprising to hear that this solo had received 1st place. Not only that, it had been given 98%, the highest marks the school had ever received. I was so grateful to Betty, because it proved that she had been inspired that day, and did have a special gift for choreography.

Being accepted into the Sadler's Wells School presented a major problem, because my parents could not afford the fees. While my father was home on leave, they applied to Bournemouth Council to ask if they could help in some way, especially as I now had the Solo Seal. However, they said that ballet was not an 'art,' and that they were therefore unable to help!

After some days of wondering what to do, my grandmother came up with the suggestion that she would sell her house in Bournemouth and go and live with her sister in New Zealand. Her idea was that she would sell the house to my mother, who would need an enormous mortgage to make the purchase, but would then be able (after needed repairs were carried out) to sell the refurbished property for a much larger sum. The difference would be hers to take us to London, and that is what happened. It was sad for us, that my grandmother should be going so far away. However, I can never be grateful enough to her for her kindness and this wonderful idea that she had, for without that I would never have had the most amazing career which was about to follow.

Chapter 4

In London at the Sadler's Wells School

Early in September 1951 my mother and I arrived at The Queen's Gate Hotel in London, though we had been told that it could only take us for two nights. However, while my mother was out flat hunting, we eventually stayed seven weeks, going from room to room as they became vacant.

The Sadler's Wells School was situated on Colet Gardens, just around the corner from Barons Court tube station. The upper and lower school shared the same building. There were three studios, two with balconies, from which one could watch the classes below. The Princess Margaret Studio was on the ground floor and to go to the other two studios, one had to pass through the glassed-in Winter Garden, where there were tables and chairs, and where all the notice boards were hung. The main offices were at this end and the Baylis Hall Studio upstairs. The Garden Room Studio looked out onto a tennis court surrounded by a garden on all sides. The canteen was only available for the lower school, so I always had to take with me whatever food I needed for the day.

For the first two weeks, all the new students were kept together in the same class, which was taken by Winifred Edwards, the senior ballet mistress, who had danced with Anna Pavlova's Company. Most days, Madam and Ailne Phillips, the ballet principal, would be sitting up on the balcony and watching our classes. At the end of this time we were to be told the class in which we would be placed.

Life at the Sadler's Wells School was tough. No matter what I did, it never seemed to be good enough in the eyes of Miss Edwards. She was continually saying that I was working too hard in the wrong way. I really wondered if I had made the right decision. There were many tears, but my mother kept positive and encouraged me to keep going.

Each day when I arrived back at the hotel, my mother and I would discuss what had been going on. She was having great difficulty in finding a suitable flat for us. In the mean time, we had to buy a wooden horse drier, on which to hang my cotton tights to dry. I needed clean ones every day, and with no central heating in the hotel, they took ages to dry.

The two weeks were now up and all the new students were waiting outside the ballet office, to find out which classes they would be placed in. When it came to my turn, Miss Edwards said 'Adams, we are going to put you in Theatre Class, but if you cannot keep up, you will go down. Next!' From then on, every time I went into class, I felt it was like having a black cloud hanging over me, and when Madam was shouting at us, banging her stick on the ground to keep us in time with the music, it seemed like the end of the world, though I did my best to realise that this difficult and trying period would pass.

Our uniform for Theatre Class was a black tunic, pink tights, a burgundy coloured two-inch wide belt with a metal clasp and a burgundy piece of net to put round our hair, like a snood. For *pas de deux* we wore a white top, with old half tutus from *Ballet Imperial*, which were kept on a pole in the ballet office.

Miss Edwards said we must prepare ourselves for class, as we would for a performance. She was always alert to anyone with dirty shoes or ribbons. She would say 'you cannot have dirty ribbons on clean tights'. Also, if they were held on with a safety pin, she would see that pin when the electric light made it shine. If our hair was not tightly held back, she would run her fingers through it and say, 'your hair is like a loose tea cosy'. I remember her once shouting down the corridor to me, just as I was going into a *pas de deux* class. 'Adams, you have a hook off your tutu. Go and replace it at once!'

In class, when changing from barre shoes to pointe shoes, she would make us do it while she counted twenty out loud. She would then proceed with the class regardless of whether we were ready or not. She would say that in this way, one would always know how long it would take to change one shoe or both. Everything she was teaching us was preparing us for the theatre.

Each morning at 9 a.m. we had to attend education classes which included history and English taught by Graham Bowles, music by Miss Perrett and art by Miss Zambra. Miss McCutcheon was the headmistress of the whole school.

The Director was Arnold Haskell and he had placed a notice on the Board: 'if you do not attend your education classes, you will not be in the performances'.

These classes were then followed at 10.25 a.m. by our first classical class which lasted until 11.35 a.m. Our teachers for Theatre Class were Madam, Ailne Phillips, Harjis Plucis, and Harold Turner. Much later, Pamela May started her teaching career by giving us classes. We then had other classes, like *Pas de deux* and Character, given by Harold Turner, Mime by Ursula Moreton, Solo and Repertory dances, by Palma Nye, and extra classes given by Winifred Edwards.

Classes with Madam were hard and demanding. She was insistent on correct placing. For *adage* she only wanted the pianist to play chords, so that we were always in the right place at the right moment. Madam was clear about floor patterns with her *enchaînement* and made sure we did what she wanted. Also, we learnt about the full dynamics of dance.

Madam demonstrated all the steps with her hands, which we were watching very carefully, then suddenly she would say 'and', and we were expected to begin. Then halfway through, she would say, 'reverse it,' and if the step had been going forward, we were then expected to continue doing it backwards. All this time her stick would be banging on the the floor, to make sure we were in time with the music. Something that I did find very helpful, was when she used illustrations to demonstrate what she wanted us to feel. One such occasion was when she said, 'imagine there is one apple in the tree and you are trying to touch it with your fingers extended forward towards it. You never will touch it, but it makes the movement come alive.' Another time was when she put her hand into her pocket and brought out her handkerchief, which she dropped on the floor in front of our hand in an *arabesque penché*. This always helped us to feel what she wanted to see in that position.

I have to say, I did not really enjoy these classes. For me, they just did not seem to flow and I felt as though every drop of dance was being pumped out of me. However, I knew I must be learning a lot and had to do my best, because my career really did lie in her hands.

Ailne Phillips, the ballet principal, was an excellent teacher, very technical and fast, which was exactly what I needed, though I found the classes difficult to do. There were very few if any personal corrections and one just had to listen to what was being said and try to make sure that one was doing it. Like Madam, she demonstrated with her hands, so that no time was lost and she accomplished every thing required in the time allowed. The stick was also there to make sure we kept up with the music. One always came away feeling that it had been a good class.

Harjis Plucis from Latvia, was the company *repetiteur* and sometimes gave us two classes in the week. He was a portly gentleman, and in the soft grey cashmere jumper he always wore, he seemed like a big bear. In broken English, he would say, 'I will be friends outside the classroom, but never in the studio.' He would start the class with the same exercise, which comprised of a number of elements, saying that if you were not warm by the end of it, you had not done it well enough.

After the barre work and coming into the centre, he would often give us a lecture, which was not appreciated by all, because one felt one was getting cold. But I knew I was learning a lot and he was the one who really taught me about balance. He would say 'take sides', 'take sides', and then explain about pulling up on the supporting side and in on the working side. This really did work, and I never heard anyone else explain it in such a clear way. I really did enjoy his classes.

An instance that happened during one of his classes, has never been forgotten. A student who was watching from the balcony in the Baylis Hall, where we were, was knitting some leg warmers and dropped her ball of wool through the railings into the studio. Mr Plucis just roared! He was absolutely furious and demanded that the student come down and fetch her wool. He said, 'nobody knits or makes notes during my classes'.

Harold Turner had been a very fine leading dancer with the company and gave a very good basic class. He was always clear about what he wanted us to do. He carried a small cane, about eighteen inches long and if the pianist, usually Mrs Evans, was playing and getting a bit carried away with her music, he would go to the piano and start tapping it with his stick until she stopped. The cane also was sent flying through the air to near our feet, if they were not stretched enough.

Mr Turner used to tease me a lot, because I found it difficult to make the back of my knees touch in first position. So he would put his hand into his pocket and produce a penny, which he then put between my knees and said 'hold it'.

Soon after arriving at the school, we were told always to read the notice board first thing in the morning and before leaving. After six weeks, there was my name on the Sadler's Wells Company notice board. Davis Theatre, Croydon. *Swan Lake*, Court Ladies – Adams. Was I on the first rung of the ladder? This news meant that I needed to go to Frizzels, the chemist at Leicester Square, who sold all the things needed to be able to put on a full greasepaint stage make-up.

The company rehearsed at the EMI building at Hammersmith, one tube stop from Barons Court. It was such a thrill to be actually there with Madam taking the rehearsals. I remember the first thing she made us do as Court Ladies was to walk across the studio through the music, not as easy as one might think, and she certainly had no patience if we did not get it right.

When it came to my first performance, there was the question of how to put on a full greasepaint make-up. I had no idea, we had not been taught, so I just had to sit next to someone experienced and follow what she was doing. It was certainly not easy – blotting out one's own eyebrows, blending all the colours together for the base, and then painting on new ones. Also, there was the question of putting on the wig correctly. Nothing like being thrown in at the deep end and having to swim!

The company was performing for one week at the Davis Theatre, Croydon, and the first performance was *Swan Lake*. My mother was able to get a ticket, and she gave me a little koala bear, as a mascot. There were several performances of *Swan Lake* that week, besides the triple bill.

This certainly brought more good news, because if I was now to be performing with the ballet and opera companies, I would receive five shillings for a walk-on part, like Court Ladies, and seven shillings and six pence if I was actually dancing.

There was progress, too, about a flat. One had just come in to the estate agent. It happened to be over the road from the hotel and belonged to a lady who was going to spend three months in Bournemouth over the winter. She was apparently being very particular about who she had to live there, but was happy when she met my mother. Also, she decided to stay on in Bournemouth for an extra month, so that was helpful for us. The flat was up eighty-four stairs and there was no lift, but very suitable for our needs. It was convenient for me to walk to Gloucester Road tube station for the school and South Kensington for Covent Garden.

This was now the most magical time of my life, actually to be on stage, dancing with the Sadler's Wells Ballet at the Royal Opera House, Covent Garden! It was the time of the seven ballerinas, Margot Fonteyn, Beryl Grey, Moira Shearer, Violetta Elvin, Rowena Jackson, Svetlana Beriosova, and Nadia Nerina, and wonderful soloists like Pamela May and Julia Farron. More opportunities soon came to be performing with the company, and I was in all the acts of the full-length ballets.

There were now dances to learn for the operas. Students from Theatre Class were chosen and these were taught at the school by Palma Nye, prior to the stage rehearsals. To be performing in *Rigoletto, Aida, A Masked Ball, Boris Godounov*, and *Orpheus* in the presence of such great singers as Kathleen Ferrier, Constance Shacklock and Nicola Rossi Lemeni, to name but a few, was amazing.

The first performance of *Rigoletto* was a Royal Gala, in the presence of Her Majesty the Queen and Princess Margaret. Just two days before, I was able to get a ticket for my mother. She was thrilled, but had to go shopping for a long evening dress. I remember it was emerald green and she looked lovely – the first time I had seen her in a long dress.

Several performances later of *Rigoletto*, the leading singer swallowed his moustache soon after he started singing 'the drinking song' from Act I. It was a new nylon one, and of course there was no build up of artifix to hold it in position. I was standing centre stage up a few steps, right behind him, when he turned his back on the audience and starting coughing towards me and trying to get it up, I cannot imagine the expression on my face! He had to leave the stage and get help from the St John's Ambulance, who were always in attendance. The orchestra just continued as normal and soon after we had our dancing part to do. As we were only needed for Act I, I don't remember hearing the rest of the story.

There always seemed to be quite a few dramas with the operas. Another happened to Rossi Lemeni who was coming from La Scala, Milan to make his debut at Covent Garden. He was due to sing the title role in Boris Godounov. However, he had to sing at the dress rehearsal in his sports jacket, because his elaborate costumes had been held up by the Customs on the French/Italian border. My mother was attending that rehearsal, and I remember her saying, that it did not matter at all about the costume, because he had such a magnificent voice.

At that time, *Aida* seemed to be in the programme frequently and for us dancers, it was a bit of a nightmare. We were slaves, and our costumes only consisted of light baggy trousers and a skimpy top, so the rest of our bodies had to be covered in wet brown make-up. We were dancing in Act I, and in Act III we were standing on top of the tomb, quite still in a position like a frieze, and the lights were low. Because of that, during Act II, we attempted to remove the wet brown, but not always successfully. There were only six hand basins in the chorus room, where the twelve of us were having to change, and more often than not, we went home with quite a lot of the wet brown still on. The last curtain was not until 10.35p.m., so no one wanted to hang around. If Harold Turner was giving our class the next day, he would always be teasing us that we had been on in *Aida* the night before and had not washed the wet brown off properly.

The last opera I was dancing in was *Orpheus*. Fredrick Ashton had choreographed the dances and they were so beautiful. Kathleen Ferrier's singing was out of this world. What a privilege to have been on stage with this wonderful artist! Regrettably however, she was only able to do five performances. At the last one, the audience were calling for her to take her calls and the only way she could make it to the front curtain was to be carried. Just a short while later, we were all so sad to hear that she had passed on.

After four months in the flat it was time to move again and my mother found a bachelor flat in Prince of Wales Terrace, off Kensington High Street. It was up seventy-six stairs and there was no lift. By now, I had certainly learnt not to forget anything that I needed. The fun and games started, when my father came home on leave and we had to buy a camp bed for me to sleep on in the sitting room. My grandmother also came over from New Zealand, during the fourteen months we were in this flat, and slept in a room in Earl's Court, and then spent the day with my mother in the flat.

It was during this visit that she suggested that we should think about buying a small house and not keep spending so much money on renting flats. She promised to help financially and said that she would probably come back to England and live with us. This seemed to be a wonderful idea, as we were not really happy living in flats, and did so miss having a garden to walk out into. As soon as my grandmother had returned to New Zealand, my mother started making inquiries and looking at suitable areas.

From February 1952 I was dancing in the following ballets which were in the repetoire, *Swan Lake, The Sleeping Beauty, Giselle, Cinderella, Sylvia, Mam'zelle Angot, Coppélia, Daphnis and Chloe, Don Juan, Don Quixote, Job, La Boutique Fantasque, Checkmate, Tiresias, The Three-Cornered Hat, Veneziana, A Mirror for Witches, Apparitions,* and *Homage to the Queen.*

All this excitement and thrill, but I was still a student in the school and seemed to be on stage every evening. The days did seem long, especially as we had to be in the education classes every morning at 9 a.m. Miss Edwards was keeping a tight check on when the company rehearsals finished, to see if we could fit in yet one more class before going directly to the Opera House.

Madam and Miss Phillips started watching our classes from the balcony again, when they were not teaching, and seemed to be discussing us students. It really was hard to live with, if I felt I had not done a good class.

One experience I shall never forget was on the last night of the old *Coppélia* production. At the half hour call, before the curtain was due to rise, I heard that I had to go on for someone who should be in the 'Dance of the Hours'. We were called on stage to allow me to have a walk through the placing, as there were twelve of us and I had not danced this before, only learnt it from the side lines. I heard Madam say to Miss Phillips, 'Who is that girl?' 'Adams' was the reply. After it was all over, Madam called out to me, 'Well done Adams, good luck.' Coming from her, this remark felt more precious than gold, and I have treasured it ever since!

Chapter 5

Joining the Sadler's Wells Ballet Company

For the company, and for us as students from the school, 1952 was a very busy year.

In the January issue of *Vogue* magazine, there was a picture of five of us from the school, taken by Cecil Beaton, the famous royal photographer. He had asked for dancers to model the latest full petticoats, and I was one of those to be chosen.

The photographs were taken at the company rehearsal studio, in Hammersmith. We wore black strapless boned tops, above petticoats, all of us wearing a different colour and type of material. Mine was black net. Our hair was neatly tied back with a black velvet band and we wore pink tights and pointe shoes. To have this opportunity of working with Cecil Beaton really was an honour.

Besides the current repertoire, we were rehearsing for a new ballet called *A Mirror for Witches*, and its first performance was on the 4th of March.

We were then rehearsing for a full-length production of *Sylvia*, a ballet with three acts. The choreographer was Frederick Ashton and the first performance took place on the 3rd of September.

Something I have never forgotten took place during one of these performances, on an evening when London was experiencing very thick smog. At that time, the scenery was stored in a warehouse opposite the back of the stage, so everything had to be kept open, while the scenery was being brought across. When the main curtains opened for this ballet, there was a gauze curtain in the front of the stage. Then when this was lifted, the smog which had collected behind it, sailed across over the orchestra pit and into the stalls. The surprised audience, wondering what had happened, suddenly started coughing.

Following soon after this was the new revised production of *Swan Lake* by Ninette de Valois, with thirty-two swans. Leslie Hurry redesigned the scenery and costumes. Frederick Ashton choreographed the *Pas de Six* in Act I, and the Neopolitan Dance in Act III, for Julia Farron and Alexander Grant. This proved to be a show-stopper. Besides dancing in all the acts, I always enjoyed being one of the six Princesses in Act III. It was a lovely dance to do. The first performance was a Royal Gala given on the 18th of December, and was danced by Beryl Grey and John Field, because Margot Fonteyn had been taken ill a few weeks beforehand.

In the new year of 1953, I was released from attending the Education classes at the school. It really was becoming too much, dancing in so many performances with the opera and ballet company and all the rehearsals as well.

From the middle of February until May, we had a ballet season, with performances every night and matinee and evening on Saturdays. Because there was no canteen in the Royal Opera House, on Saturdays between the two shows, they would sometimes give us sandwiches and coffee in the Crush Bar.

During stage rehearsals, at a break, we would be allowed to go up to the top of the Royal Opera House, behind the back row of the Gallery, where someone would have an urn of coffee. The only problem with this was that by the time we made it up there, it was time to go back down.

On the 4th of March I received the most wonderful news – something that I had dreamed of for so long. Mr Hughes, the company manager, offered me a contract to join the Sadler's Wells Ballet Company at Covent Garden. He also said that I would be going with the company on their third tour of the United States and Canada.

There were just three of us out of sixteen in Theatre Class, to be chosen at that time. However, three more did join later. Mr Hughes gave me the contract and all the papers for a passport and asked for everything to be returned as soon as possible. The next couple of days were hectic, arranging for a medical examination and passport photos to be taken. However, everything was done and returned to Mr Hughes as requested.

On the following Saturday Miss Phillips told us that from now on we must attend company classes. There had been occasions when we had done so before, but that was because of rehearsals. Now, however, it was official. These classes were taken by Madam, Mr Plucis and Miss Phillips, who had just been promoted to the position of Madam's personal assistant. It was so nice to have the continuity of having the same teachers, because the company classes were much larger than the ones at the school.

This change in the organisation meant there were other moves as well. Ursula Moreton, who had been Director of Sadler's Wells Theatre Ballet, would now take over the job of ballet principal at the school. Peggy van Praagh, who had been the ballet mistress, would take her place as director, and Barbara Fewster move into the position of ballet mistress.

Before the curtain went up during performances, one would always find Madam, Miss Phillips and Mr Plucis there on stage. Mr Plucis was like a father figure and would go to anyone, from the ballerinas down to the newest member of the corps de ballet, to offer help if he felt they needed it, when trying out steps. He would also be seen giving Margot Fonteyn a warm up before all her performances, at the back of the stage.

During performances, Madam would be sitting in her box, the one nearest to the stage, on the grand tier level. From there, she could just walk down the stairs and through the pass door to the stage, so she was always near at hand.

On the 16th of March the company was treated to several guest performances, given by Alicia Markova, in *Giselle* and *Swan Lake* Act II. They were her last appearances before she retired. I happened to meet Madam on my way home and she remarked, 'What a wonderful artist she is!'

Margot Fonteyn had been back with us for a while, though she had not found it easy to regain her strength. Now the time had come for her first performance, which was to be on the 18th of March, in the ballet *Apparitions*, when she would wear the most beautiful ball gown. It was an outstanding success and it was so exciting to be on stage at the end, when all the flowers starting raining down from the gallery slips and the front corners of the stalls circle. To see her standing alone at the end, taking calls amid this carpet of flowers was a sight to behold.

In the middle of March my grandmother arrived back from New Zealand. It was very convenient timing because my mother, after much searching, had seen a small house which had just come on the market, at Southfields, near Wimbledon. We were all able to arrange to go and see it together. It had a lovely 100 foot garden and was very convenient for the District Line, which was only a few minutes walk away. We all agreed that this was the right place for us and decided to go ahead with the purchase.

For the past month we had been rehearsing another new ballet, *Veneziana*, which had its first performance on the 9th of April.

Around this time, Baron, the ballet photographer, chose five dancers from the corps de ballet for press photographs for our forthcoming tour of America. I was one of those and we had to go to his studio in Park Lane. This all made it feel that the tour was actually going to happen, although there were still nineteen weeks to go. Two weeks later, we started to rehearse *Homage to the Queen*, a ballet to be shown on the evening of Coronation Day. Frederick Ashton was the choreographer, and it was all about the four elements. The music was by Malcolm Arnold, and the scenery by Oliver Messel. The Queen of the Earth was danced by Nadia Nerina with her Consort Alexis Rassine and her six Attendants, plus a *Pas de Six*; the Queen of the Waters was danced by Violetta Elvin with her Consort John Hart and her eight Attendants, plus a *Pas de Trois*; the Queen of Fire was danced by Beryl Grey with her Consort John Field and the Spirit of Fire, Alexander Grant, plus a *Pas de Quatre*; the Queen of the Air was danced by Margot Fonteyn with her Consort Michael Somes and her Attendants, six girls and six boys. It was such a thrill for me to be one of these Attendants with Fonteyn.

On the 15th of May we moved into our new home, which proved to be a very happy and convenient place for all of us.

The 2nd of June was the Coronation of Queen Elizabeth II, and my family and I were invited by the bank manager and his wife to their flat over the bank, to watch the proceedings on their television. We were so pleased, because at that time we did not have a television and it was wonderful to see the Coronation as it was actually happening.

Later in the day I had to go to the Royal Opera House for the performance. It was a lovely programme, starting with *Swan Lake* Act II, *Façade*, and then finishing with *Homage to the Queen*. After a very exciting day, the performance went well and turned out to be a most memorable occasion.

It was now necessary to start thinking about the clothes I would need for the American tour. Very hot weather in California and freezing cold in Chicago. I needed to have evening clothes, suitable to wear to the receptions we had to attend after the performances.

Also, some comfortable things to wear for the long train journeys. It really had to be thought out, to the last detail.

We were only allowed to have one large suitcase, which must not exceed a certain weight. We also had to have a grip which must contain our practice clothes, in case we were separated from our cases and needed to go to the theatre for a class or rehearsal.

We had to keep our hair long enough to be able to do a classical hair style, as the only false pieces we were lent from the wardrobe were a bunch of curls, and two sets of four ringlets. With these, we were able to do a variety of things, on top of our hair, after it had been put up in a bun or pleat.

As mentioned earlier, tights had been a problem and we were now able to buy pink fishnet ones from Freed's. These were, however, very hard on the feet and we had to wear sockets inside.

Pointe shoes were rationed to four pairs a month, which was barely enough. They were often like paper when I had finished with them.

It was now the end of June and our holiday had arrived. I went to Bournemouth with my mother for a couple of weeks to see family and friends. It was wonderful to be able to walk on the sand and smell the sea air again.

After the holiday the company had one week of classes before starting three weeks of rehearsals. Then on the 24th of August we began two weeks of performances at the Royal Opera House, prior to leaving for the United States and Canada.

Chapter 6

The Company's third tour of the USA and Canada

On Sunday the 6th of September 1953 the company flew from Heathrow Airport in a BOAC Stratocruiser. It was certainly overloaded – there were seventy-two of us, and seven had their seats in the cocktail lounge. It was a charter flight so we were free to move around as we pleased. With us were Ailne Phillips, Harjis Plucis and Frederick Ashton, who told all the ballerinas that they must have the bunks to sleep in during the night.

We stopped off at Shannon airport where we were given dinner, and then back on the plane to fly to Gander, Newfoundland. Unfortunately the cooling system broke down and it was extremely hot. The stop at Gander was only for half an hour and then we were off again to New York. However, soon after receiving breakfast, for which we had been waiting a long time, we encountered a severe storm. For the next several hours, we were just going up and down, until we were closer to New York and the plane was able to have a good landing.

By the time we arrived on Monday we had been travelling for seventeen hours. Feeling rather worse for wear, we were led off the plane by Margot Fonteyn and greeted by a large group of press photographers. After customs etc., we were driven in two large buses through the streets of New York, with a police escort, sirens blazing, to our various hotels. The hotel where I was staying was on 7th Avenue. It was just ten minutes walk down Broadway to the Metropolitan Opera House where we were performing.

On Tuesday, with several others, I went for a walk in Central Park and took a number of photographs with my Brownie box camera. Of course, they were all in black and white, because there was no colour at this time, except at a price we could not afford. We tried to become familiar with our surroundings before going to the theatre for a class with Madam. She gave us everything in that class, including pointe work. I don't think we really felt that we had recovered from that long journey.

A lady had come to the theatre to take orders for 'Danskin' tights. These were the ones that Fonteyn had told us about, as she had been wearing them in London. As this lady had such a large order, she was able to get them for us at a much cheaper price. They turned out to be just wonderful to wear, after those awful hard fishnets.

On Thursday, after an early class, we started to rehearse for some of the ballets that we had brought with us: *Swan Lake, The Sleeping Beauty*, and *Homage to the Queen*. The other ballets to be included were *Sylvia, Giselle, Don Juan, Daphnis and Chloe, Les Patineurs, The Shadow*, and *Checkmate*.

On Sunday, we had our first performance of *Swan Lake* with Fonteyn and Somes, and what a tremendous ovation they received. Afterwards, we had to attend a reception at the Waldorf Astoria. All the ballerinas and soloists were in long evening dresses, except for Fonteyn, who was wearing Dior's latest short evening dress, with low back. I must say, I was happy with the deep green taffeta dress that I had taken with me.

The following day we were free and as I had been given an introduction to some friends in New Jersey, they invited me and a couple of others to visit them. They came to fetch us in their car, so we had a good view of all the countryside as we went along, and we really did enjoy a happy relaxing day in a family home.

From now on we had eight performances a week, with two on Saturday and two on Sunday. Our day off was on Monday. I found it quite a challenge, because besides the performances, we also had classes and rehearsals every day.

On our second Monday off the whole company had been invited by Allen Talbot to 'Smoke Rise,' the Place for Ideal Country Living. It too, was in New Jersey. We were all taken in large coaches and were able to enjoy the countryside. The grounds were magnificent, with a beautiful lake. Some went swimming, others went out in a canoe or a rowing boat. That day turned out to be very hot, so to be near the water was most welcome, and we did have a lovely time.

Sadly, we heard that Madam had to leave us and return to London for a serious operation. When I said good bye to her, she said that she hoped to be back with us by Christmas. I had become so used to her being around and really did miss her very much.

On another free Monday I was invited with a couple of others to go down the Hudson River, in a sight-seeing boat round Manhattan Island. That really was exciting, being able to have all the important places pointed out to us. The two friends who took us were very keen on the ballet. As the husband had to travel around the States a lot on business, they arranged to be in a number of the places where we were performing. So we were able to meet up with them again later.

On yet another day, I went up the Empire State Building, at that time the tallest building in the world. At the very top, besides having a fantastic view and being able to take lots of photographs, one could also make a recording of one's voice, and send it away from there. I decided to make one for my parents, with a Christmas message, as this was to be my first time away from home.

On Sunday the 11th of October after being in New York for five weeks, we had our last two performances of *The Sleeping Beauty*. The evening one with Fonteyn was absolutely fabulous, the audience just did not want to stop applauding. Frederick Ashton went on stage in place of Madam, to say a few words. It was then that we really felt sad about leaving.

Monday was our last day in New York. With some of the other company members, I was so pleased to be able to arrange to have some photographs taken by the famous ballet photographer, Maurice Seymour.

On the Tuesday, we had to be ready early, with cases in the hall by 8 a.m. We were leaving at 9 a.m., to go by bus to the station to board our train for Philadelphia. This was the train that would be taking us around the United States and Canada. On the back, was a large notice: Sadler's Wells Ballet Special. I must say, it was not the most up-to-date train at that time, but we got used to it over the next few weeks.

It took us nearly two hours to get to Philadelphia and when we arrived at our hotel, we found that the theatre, the Philadelphia Academy of Music, was just over the road. There were several good places for us to eat nearby. We had a class at 7p.m. and then a performance of *Sylvia* to follow.

We stayed there for five days, doing six performances, which included two on Wednesday. Our last one was a matinee on Saturday. The Philadelphia Orchestra were giving a concert in the evening and a number of us were able to get tickets for it, which was wonderful.

We were so glad to have this opportunity to hear them and it filled in the time until midnight, when our buses were coming to take us to the station.

After quite a good sleep on the train, we arrived in Boston in the middle of Sunday morning and were driven to our hotel. Sorting out the luggage was always the first thing we had to do, and then I found a map, because there were a number of places that I was most interested to see. My roommate and I set out first of all to find the theatre where we were performing, the Boston Opera House. Then we continued walking around finding all the places of interest and looking for good places to eat.

On Monday, after the performance, the company was all invited to a private supper party, which was very pleasant. The British Ambassador was there and also the press, and the next day several of us from the company found our pictures in the newspapers.

I really did enjoy being in Boston and able to visit so many of the places that were of interest to me. While there for six days, from the 19th to the 24th of October, we gave eight performances, with two on Thursday and two on Saturday.

After the last evening performance and packing up, we were taken straight to the station, where our train was waiting. By now I had found a way to swing myself up to my top bunk. This was certainly better than having to call for the porter to bring the steps every time. It was not long before others were doing the same.

After finishing with an evening performance, it took all our stage crew until 3 a.m. to load the scenery and all the boxes aboard the train before we could leave. This became the usual procedure. After the initial jolt, we knew we were moving and could then go to sleep until the next morning.

We were now on our way to cross the border into Canada, where we would be performing at the Maple Leaf Gardens in Toronto, just for three days, the 27th to the 29th of October.

We arrived early on Monday morning, our free day. As soon as we had checked into the hotel we were all taken by buses to Niagara Falls and what a wonderful day we had there, appreciating all the amazing scenery and making use of our cameras.

We soon discovered that the theatre was an Ice Hockey Stadium. It was not too bad, even though a stage had to be built especially for us on top of the ice. Our changing room was in an enormous tent with all the girls together including Fonteyn. When the boys needed to change, they had to go through part of the audience to get to their changing area. We never really knew quite what to expect in the theatres where we performed.

Each day in Toronto seemed to be full and quite hectic. Either it was a luncheon, or a tea or a supper party we had to attend. The people there were most generous with their hospitality, but we had to keep some energy for the performances!

After our last performance of *Swan Lake* we travelled overnight to Montreal. There we were only staying one night in a hotel which seemed very modern, and I was on the 22nd floor at the very top. From there, I had a magnificent view over the city.

That night we had a performance of *Swan Lake*. The theatre was awful! Again, the stage had been built on top of an ice rink, and we were told that during Act II, it had slipped a couple of feet towards the audience. The cold air seemed to be coming up between the floorboards and we were beginning to lose all feeling in our feet and legs. The best thing was the party afterwards, given by the Mayor. It really was one of the best of the whole tour. The following day, Saturday, we had two performances of *The Sleeping Beauty*, after which we were taken back to the train.

Our journey now would be overnight and through the following day, until we arrived at 6p.m. on Sunday at our next destination, which was East Lancing. There we were giving two performances, on the Monday and Tuesday.

We stayed at the Kellogg Centre, a college campus which was a place for further education, miles away from anywhere and surrounded by trees, playing fields and a river. It was wonderful to have so much fresh air. We just had to make sure that we did not miss their restaurant times, otherwise it was a twenty minute brisk walk to the nearest drug store to get a meal.

We had class and rehearsed at the Centre before the buses took us to the theatre, the College Auditorium, in East Lancing. That evening the programme included a triple bill: *Checkmate, Don Juan,* and *The Sleeping Beauty* Act III.

As we were leaving the next day we had to vacate our rooms early, before having class and rehearsal, and were given a room in which to put all our bags and relax before the performance. It was not nearly large enough for our requirements and a number of us were lying on the floor trying to get some rest. Our performance that night included *Swan Lake* Act II, *The Shadow* and *Sleeping Beauty* Act III.

Our next port of call was Detroit, staying just for one night and giving two performances at the Masonic Auditorium.

We then received some not very encouraging news. There was apparently no hotel accommodation available in Lafayette, our next stop, and we would have to spend the next three nights in the train. This meant that we would not be able to get to our suitcases.

Our arrival at Lafayette was around 11 a.m. and the first thing we were told was to put our watches back one hour. I had just got up and on going to the ladies room, found that the water had run out. Most people were still asleep, but I found several others who were prepared to come with me and see if we could find somewhere to clean our teeth.

We got off the train and walked out of the station. Eventually we found a shop and after going in and explaining the situation, we were allowed to use their staff room. That did made us feel better and we returned to the train refreshed. However, we then heard that there would be no more water until we arrived in Minneapolis, our next port of call.

The theatre where we were giving two performances was the Purdue Hall of Music in the University. The changing room was rather small, only nineteen places for thirty of us, including the soloists, plus the students who were extras, being Court Ladies. So it turned out to be a very tight squeeze. The two friends I had met in New York attended both performances and after the second one, they invited me to have a meal with them, which certainly helped me to forget all the inconveniences we had encountered in Lafayette.

Arriving at the station, we realised that our train had been changed for a slightly smarter one, probably because we were going to have to stay in the train for so long. This solved the water problem. Every so often, the train stopped for three minutes, when we could get off and enjoy some exercise.

As we travelled alongside the Mississippi river, the rail track seemed so close to the water that I felt as though I was in a boat. On the other side of the train, was a road with houses and people came out to wave to us.

We arrived in Minneapolis at 5.30p.m. on Sunday the 8th of November and stayed there for three nights. This was another university, miles away from the town, and we had to eat with the students at the Union Building. Buses had to take us to the theatre, the Northrop Auditorium, where we gave three performances.

On Tuesday the 10th we had a fancy dress party, to celebrate the fact that we were half way through the tour. Frederick Ashton was Greta Garbo and looked marvellous – in fact, he won a prize. Ailne Phillips was a Spanish Lady, Pauline Claydon was a doll from *Guys and Dolls* and Philip Chatfield was a Notice Board, covered in all company notices. That really was hilarious and made everyone laugh. The party was lovely and enjoyed by all.

On Wednesday after our last performance, we went for a meal before boarding our train to take us into Canada again. This time we were heading for Winnipeg, where we were expecting to see snow. I was so glad to have been able to buy some ear muffs because we were already beginning to feel the cold.

We arrived the following morning – no snow – and stayed for two nights. The theatre was the Winnepeg Auditorium where we were giving four performances.

We were now back on the train for three nights and two days. This journey would take us through the Canadian Rockies to Vancouver. What fantastic scenery. The sun was so bright, glistening on the snow-covered mountains, that we had to wear sun glasses. All day long we were treated to this wonderful vista and the lakes looked so beautiful.

On the Monday evening we had an experience which was to hold us up for a number of hours. We had just stopped to cool the engine down for a few minutes, when there was a landslide onto the rail track, just in front of the engine. If the train had gone any further, we would have been off the rails. There were seventeen coaches on this train and we were travelling on a single track, with high mountains on one side and a sheer drop down to the valley on the other side. A message had to be sent for helpers to clear the track. In fact this hold up made us eight hours late arriving in Vancouver, and we had a performance of *Swan Lake* that night.

We arrived on Tuesday the 17th of November around 10.30 a.m. It was pouring with rain and this continued throughout our stay. Buses were there to take us to our hotel for four nights. We were able to have class and rehearse at the B.C. School of Dancing nearly next door, which was very helpful. We were performing at the Orpheum Theatre, eight performances in five days, and there seemed to be plenty of things going on to keep us all alert.

On the third day, during *Homage*, Violetta Elvin injured herself and had to hobble off the stage. The orchestra naturally kept playing, and Avril Navarre, who was standing next to me in the wings, just looked right and left and said, 'I had better go on,' and with that she was away, making up a solo as she went along. Julia Farron then danced Violetta's next solo. In the meantime, Svetlana Beriosova who was the understudy and watching from out front, came back stage. She managed to get on tights, shoes and tutu, before finishing off the final promenade round the stage. She then took all the calls with the others. Sadly Violetta was unable to dance with us any more on the tour.

On the fourth day we had a matinee and evening performance. Violetta should have been dancing *Giselle* in the evening, but Anne Heaton had to go on instead. She was only told the day before, which happened to be her birthday, and she was so thrilled to be called upon in this emergency. She had not danced this role before and was not due to do so until the London season. In spite of the brief notice, she gave an amazing and absolutely wonderful performance.

After two performances on the fifth day, we were taken from the hotel at 12.30 a.m. to go through customs, as we were now leaving Canada. I passed through very quickly with Svetlana and we were able to get on the train early and go to bed. However, it took until 3.30 a.m. before everyone else was through and the train could leave for Seattle, our next port of call.

It was now Sunday the 22nd of November and when we arrived at 7.45 a.m. we had to leave the train straight away. This was not really appreciated after the late get away the night before. However, the buses were waiting to take us to the hotel where we were staying for three nights. After having breakfast in the hotel coffee shop, my roommate and I went up to our room and slept until after 2p.m., trying to catch up on some sleep. Fortunately we did not have a performance that day.

The theatre where we were performing for the next three nights was the Civic Auditorium. We gave two triple bills and one performance of *Swan Lake*. The theatre was quite a distance from the hotel and buses had to take us to and fro. This gave us an opportunity to see all the Christmas decorations in the shops and in the streets.

After an overnight journey, we arrived in Portland at 8.15 a.m. on Thursday the 26th of November. The buses were waiting and took us to our hotel for a two-night stay. Checking in and collecting our luggage always took time. Then breakfast and trying to get more sleep before class in the afternoon. This was held at a place just around the corner from the hotel, so that was easy to get to. Later, we were taken by bus to the Public Auditorium, the theatre where we were giving four performances.

Our travels now took us down the West Coast and what fantastic views we had from the train, all day Sunday. We arrived at Oakland around 10.30p.m. and then had to cross the bay by ferry to San Francisco, which took half an hour. To see all the lights of the city at that time of night was truly amazing.

On arrival at the hotel we found that a large bowl of fresh fruit had been placed in all our rooms, a gift from the manager. What a wonderful sight! I had never seen anything like that before because of the rationing. It was a reminder to me to send home several parcels of tins of Del Monte fruit, which we were not able to get at that time.

We stayed in San Francisco for seven nights and at last I could feel a little more settled and have more normality to my days.

The weather now was like summer and as we had a free day on Monday, one of the company suggested that six of us should hire a car and drive all round Oakland and San Francisco. We left at 10.30 a.m. and drove over the Golden Gate Bridge and up to the top of Mount Tamalpais, where we had a superb view of the city. We all had a wonderful day, arriving back around 9.30p.m. We were so pleased that we took the opportunity because from then on the week was very full.

The War Memorial Opera House was the theatre where we were giving eight performances. It was a wonderful theatre with a large stage, like the one at the Opera House in Covent Garden. In some places on the tour, we had experienced quite small stages. The dressing rooms were lovely too and so well equipped. We were now showing *Sylvia*, which we had not given since Boston, and also because of having the space we could do the full *Sleeping Beauty*.

After a happy week there we travelled over night to Los Angeles, arriving on Monday morning, the 7th of December. We were all staying at the famous Ambassador Hotel, where so many film stars stay. This was to be a treat for us for nine nights, the longest stay in one place since New York. The hotel was very special and had absolutely everything that one could possibly wish for.

We opened at the Shrine Auditorium, on Tuesday the 8th of December, with the larger version of *Swan Lake*. By now we had two versions, one for the smaller stages and one for the larger ones, and we really had to concentrate hard to remember which version we were actually doing!

After this performance we were taken back to the hotel to get ready for the Ballet Ball, to which the whole company had been invited. We were all sitting at various tables with society people who had attended the performance. The food was excellent and the dancing good fun.

We gave two more performances of *Swan Lake* on the Wednesday and Thursday evenings, *The Sleeping Beauty* on the Friday and on the Saturday matinee and evening. Two different programmes of the triple bill were given for the Sunday matinee and evening.

I was very fortunate because I was contacted by some friends, who were there to meet my every need. When I was free for lunch they took me to visit many famous places, including the Hollywood Bowl.

Our last two performances on the Tuesday and Wednesday were of *Sylvia* and both received a tremendous ovation.

What an exciting time that had been for me and now we had to move on and make our way to Denver.

It took us two nights and one and a half days in our train before we arrived on Friday the 18th of December at 1.45p.m. We had been expecting to see snow. However, the sun was shining and it was quite warm until the evening. As we had to give a performance that night, it was quite a quick turn round to get organised, before the buses came at 6.30p.m. to take us to the theatre, the Denver Auditorium.

After the last performance on Saturday we were back on the train for another long journey, this time to Chicago, known as the windy city. It was not long before we found that to be true.

We arrived on Monday the 21st of December when it was snowing, but the snow only lasted a few days. However, it was freezing cold. I had not experienced any thing as extreme as that before and the 'chill factor' of the wind made it feel even worse.

We were performing at the Civic Opera House, from Tuesday the

22nd of December to Sunday the 3rd of January. This was a very strange theatre. It was divided in half. On one side the ballet was performing, while on the other side was a circus. So when making our way to the changing room, it was not unusual to bump into an elephant!

The good news was that Madam was now back with us. I saw her come out of the hotel lift and she gave me one of her happy smiles.

During the first week we gave three performances of *Swan Lake*, then on the Friday it was Christmas Day. Together with some others, I was invited out for lunch. That was really very special and we were given such a wonderful time. Then we were back to the theatre in time for the performance of *The Sleeping Beauty* that night.

The next day, Saturday, we gave two more performances of that ballet, and on Sunday, two different programmes of a triple bill. During the rest of our stay, we gave eight more performances, which included *Giselle* and *Sylvia*. The latter was our final performance and it was given a tremendous reception.

How we had appreciated being in one place for thirteen days. However, that was now to change and we would again be making a number of short stops. During the next week, we travelled to Atlanta, Birmingham and New Orleans. Then we embarked on another long train journey, two nights and a day, to take us to Washington.

Because of heavy snow, we arrived later than expected, on Monday the 11th of January. When we got into the buses to take us to our hotel, they had to be pushed before we could move. When I took my clothes out of my suitcase, they were freezing cold, they must have been standing around outdoors for some time.

Talking about luggage, we often saw our cases being thrown from the train onto the platform, and they really were very battered and often did not survive. Even mine, which was supposed to be strong, had a large dent in it and the corners looked very much the worse for wear.

It was now necessary to do some ironing as we had a reception the next day. Living out of a suitcase was not much fun and everything became very creased, even using masses of tissue paper. Oh, how we could have done with some plastic bags!

On Tuesday a class was scheduled for 10 a.m. followed by a rehearsal. However, the room we were supposed to have was not free and the stage at the theatre had not yet been set. So the whole thing had to be abandoned. Later, when we did get to the Loew's Capitol Theatre, we found it was a cinema, and the stage was really too small.

We were due to perform *The Shadow, Homage* and *Les Patineurs*. After the first ballet, the interval had to be extended and lasted over three-quarters of an hour, with the audience becoming very restless. The set for *Homage* just would not fit into the small space and Madam was not at all pleased, I think she wanted to cancel it. However, we did proceed, but there was hardly any room to move. After the performance the company had been invited to the British Embassy for a party, and we were all given a good meal, and had an enjoyable time. Before leaving Washington we gave three more performances.

Our next stop was Cleveland and after that Pittsburgh, where we really were coming towards the end of the tour.

The whole experience had been quite amazing and certainly one that I shall never forget. I especially remember the wonderful feeling of friendship and team work throughout the company, from the ballerinas down to the youngest member of the corps de ballet. To be living out of one suitcase for such a long time was an experience in itself, as was coping with the extremes in temperature and also dealing with all the strange times for eating and sleeping. Everywhere we went the audiences were so appreciative and enthusiastic, clapping when we least expected it. I think it roused everyone to do of their very best, and the boys seemed to jump higher, and turn faster, as if striving to break a world record.

Baltimore was our last port of call. We arrived the next morning at 10.30 a.m. on Friday the 22nd of January and there was snow everywhere. From the buses we could see that we were staying near the shops, so were able to do some last minute shopping.

The theatre where we were performing was the Lyric. The programme for that night was a triple bill, and on Saturday two performances of *Swan Lake*. How exciting was that last performance! The audience was so enthusiastic and obviously did not want us to leave.

It was then back to the train for our last journey to New York, before flying home after giving one hundred and thirty-six performances over nineteen weeks. We arrived at 8.30 a.m. and had to leave the train and find somewhere to have breakfast. As we then had time to spare, in the afternoon we were able to go to a performance of the

New York City Ballet, which was a special treat for us.

Those members of the company in *Les Patineurs* had to perform on television that evening, which we were able to watch. That was apparently the reason why we had to wait around all day before our flight.

The buses came to collect us at 10p.m. to go to the airport for a flight at midnight. What rejoicing, we were on our way. The first stop was Gander, Newfoundland. It was supposed to be a short stop, but we landed with only three engines. We were told the stop would be just for one hour but when it turned out to be for much longer, we were taken to some huts, where we could try and get some sleep. I remember the water in the basin was brown. Twelve and a half hours later, we made our way to the aircraft down a path between two walls of snow, banked on either side of us, and well above my height. The snow was coming down quite heavily as we took off, but we were happy to be on our way again.

We arrived in London on Tuesday the 26th of January at 5.30 a.m. My parents had followed the tour on a map of the United States and Canada, using a red ribbon and little paper flags on pins, and they were both at the airport to meet me. What a happy reunion that was! Though both mentally and physically demanding, the extensive tour of these beautiful countries had been an immensely enjoyable and worthwhile experience, but it was wonderful to see my parents again after such a long time away. My heart danced with delight as the glorious realisation dawned upon me – 'I'm home!'

Chapter 7

A Midsummer Night's Dream tour of the USA and Canada and future career plans

The company now had two weeks holiday before starting classes and rehearsals for the season at the Royal Opera House, from the 23rd of February until the 16th of June. It was just so wonderful to be back in the studio for class, rather than being on a stage with a rake.

We opened with *The Sleeping Beauty* and several days later there was a new revised version of *Coppélia* by Ninette de Valois. That season also included another full length ballet, *Cinderella*, plus a number of shorter ballets. We were also rehearsing the new production of *Firebird*. To be there, watching Tamara Karsavina and Serge Grigoriev at the rehearsals, was a sheer inspiration.

On the 17th of June we took the train and then ferry from Harwich, over to The Hook of Holland, for a week of performances during the Holland Festival. We stayed in various hotels in Scheveningen around the famous Kurhaus and it was there that we had all our meals. Four performances were given in Amsterdam and three in The Hague. The ballets we took with us, were *Swan Lake, The Shadow, Homage to the Queen* and *The Three Cornered Hat*. We came home on Wednesday the 23rd of June and then had three performances at the Royal Opera House, prior to our summer holiday.

* * *

During the past year or so, Michael Benthall, director of the Old Vic Company, had been working on a new lavish production of Shakespeare's *A Midsummer Night's Dream*. The leading roles were to be played by Moira Shearer, Robert Helpmann and Stanley Holloway, the other parts played by famous actors and actresses.

Scenery and costumes were by Robin and Christopher Ironside. Choreography was by Robert Helpmann with the Nocturne arranged by Frederick Ashton and the symphony orchestra under the direction of Hugo Rignold.

Barbara Fewster, who had been ballet mistress for the Sadler's Well Theatre Ballet, left to be the ballet mistress. The corps de ballet consisted of eighteen girls and six boys, and together with three others, I left the Sadler's Wells Company and joined this production.

The premiere was to be on Tuesday the 31st of August at the 1954 Edinburgh Festival. After a two week season at the Empire Theatre, the company would fly off to the United States and Canada, for a similar tour to that of the Sadler's Wells Ballet. However, instead of visiting twenty-four places, it would only call at thirteen and be one month shorter in length.

On the 26th of July we started classes and rehearsals at the Old Vic Theatre and after nearly a month of rehearsals, on Sunday the 22nd of August we travelled up to Edinburgh by train. I had to arrange my own lodgings and they were with a family who were very pleasant and did their best to make my stay with them a happy one.

As we were not going to be giving any performances in London, I asked the family if it would be possible for my mother to stay for the last three days, as there was a double bed in my room. Happily, they agreed. It was not easy to get any tickets, because the performances were all sold out. However, I was able to get a return ticket in the stalls for one night and a standing ticket at the back of the balcony for another. It was really lovely for my mother to be able to see the production and for her to be able to see us off.

During our first week in Edinburgh for rehearsals, the Sadler's Wells Ballet were there too, performing at the Empire Theatre and I was able to watch a number of performances from the wings and some from out front. It was wonderful to see *Firebird* on stage, after being in all the rehearsals before the holidays. I saw Madam and she asked me how I was getting on. I also saw Ailne Phillips and Harjis Plucis. Together with most of the company, they all came to watch one of our stage rehearsals.

Both companies' performances at the Empire Theatre were a great success. In our case, for the first time ever, all the scenery was able to be folded flat and put into a plane. It arrived in New York within twenty-four hours of the curtain closing at the last performance.

On Monday the 13th of September we flew from Prestwick Airport to Iceland where we were due to board the plane that was bringing Robert Helpmann, Michael Benthall and two others from London. Unfortunately, it arrived on only three engines, so there was a considerable delay while the problem was resolved.

When we arrived in New York on the Tuesday afternoon, I found that the hotel was not as near to the Metropolitan Opera House as the one I had stayed at before. After trying the hotel restaurant, it was decided not to use it again and before long, members of the company were asking me where there were good places to eat. Fortunately, a Howard Johnson restaurant was nearby and I could assure them that it was always good and not too expensive. In the end it became our meeting place.

The next day, Wednesday, Robert Helpmann called for a rehearsal on stage at 11 a.m. even before we had a class. He then proceeded to change the whole of the Scherzo. For some reason he was not happy with it in Edinburgh.

I was soon in touch with my friends in New Jersey and over the weekend I had permission to stay with them for a night in their home. It was just so lovely to meet up with them again.

We opened at the Metropolitan Opera House on Tuesday the 21st of September and the audience was very enthusiastic. Afterwards the Duchess of Kent came round back stage to greet us. She looked really lovely. Then we all had to get ready and take taxis to the reception being given at the Waldorf Astoria.

After giving nearly three weeks of performances in New York, eight each week, it was time to move on and we made our way to Philadelphia. There we gave four performances before returning to New York for four more at The Met.

Negotiations were still going on to find a theatre in which to perform in Boston at the end of the tour. However, we were told that it was not going to be possible and that we would be finishing the tour in Montreal on the 20th of December.

Once again we were back on our train, with a notice on the last carriage telling everyone that we were the Old Vic Company. We then made our way to Indiana and Minneapolis, before having a very long train journey to San Francisco. We arrived there on Tuesday the 26th of October and stayed twelve nights, giving seventeen performances.

It was there that I was able to meet up with friends again and was taken to some wonderful places, like the famous Redwood Forest. The friends who took me said that if ever they had a problem that needed working out, they would always go there and receive the answer. The peace and quiet that one felt was quite indescribable and I really understood what they meant. To have the opportunity to visit and experience all these wonderful places was so special.

This was followed by a short stop at Sacramento, for two performances, before going to Los Angeles, where we arrived on Wednesday the 10th of November, for thirteen nights. It was there that I was given permission to stay with some friends I had met before. Their home was up in the Hollywood Hills and from my room I could see all over Los Angeles. Of course I was spoiled but was so grateful to have this time with them away from the hotel. Again I was taken to some amazing places and I was very grateful to my friends for looking after me so well and seeing that I was always at the theatre in good time.

From there we had another long journey in our train, three nights and two and a half days, to Chicago. It was on these long journeys that we began to get to know the other members travelling with us. It really was like being with three companies, actors, dancers and musicians. On these occasions, Stanley Holloway would organise a sing-song in the evenings with some of the musicians and this was something we all enjoyed.

In Chicago, we experienced a complete change of temperature. After swimming in a pool in Palm Springs, now it was on with the earmuffs, warm boots and thick winter coat. We arrived on the 24th of November and stayed for twelve nights, giving fifteen performances.

It was lovely for me to see again the friends I had visited on the last tour, and once more, they gave me such a welcome and were so generous with their hospitality.

On Tuesday the 6th of December we left for two more short stops, at East Lancing and Detroit.

The advantage of this tour was that having only one production, we were free, apart from our daily class and the occasional rehearsal, to visit places of interest, which was a wonderful opportunity and so thrilling.

Barbara Fewster had given us some excellent classes throughout the tour and we were so grateful to her for keeping us up to performance standard on a tour like this, especially when classes had to be held on stage.

We were now in the final week and going into Canada. There were three performances in Toronto at the Maple Leaf Gardens and then three at the Forum Ice Rink in Montreal.

The tour had now been completed and we flew from Montreal on Monday the 20th of December. We had heard about the bad weather England was having at that time. However, we had a good flight, arriving on the Tuesday and I was so glad to be greeted by my parents.

On the way home, they said they were sorry, but hoped I would not mind if they gave me my Christmas present early. Being so tired, I think I said, 'do you have to?'

When we arrived at the house, within a few minutes, a large box was presented to me, with a red ribbon round it. As I untied it and lifted the lid, out jumped a fawn pug puppy. It was just three months old. My parents had cared for it since it was six weeks old. 'Strauby' was his name and he was absolutely wonderful, no wonder he had to make his presence known at that moment.

* * *

One evening during our stay in New York, while I was quietly reading, it suddenly came to me so clearly that teaching ballet was what I wanted to do with my life. From that moment on, I had no desire to further my dancing career. I still had the rest of the tour to enjoy, but as the weeks and months passed by, the feeling just became stronger. I had such a desire to give, to pass on to others, that love of dance which had always inspired me.

I had mentioned this to my mother in letters and during our journey home from the airport we talked about it. She was very supportive but said 'you do realise that we are unable to help you financially'. This I already knew would be the case.

My first plan was to go and talk it over with Madam, so in the new year I telephoned to make an appointment to see her. After I had explained my thoughts and feelings, she said 'don't be so ridiculous, you are far too young and should go on dancing'. Whereupon she got up from the desk, turned her back on me and walked away. The thought that came to me was, 'this requires a quick exit' so after thanking her, I left the office.

I felt absolutely devastated and when I arrived home, my mother and I just walked down the garden to try and clear my thinking. I assured her that the desire to teach was strong and that I had no doubt about it. My mother said, if you feel so sure, then just leave it for about three weeks and after that ring up and make another appointment. The thought of making another appointment with Madam was daunting, as I knew what a busy person she was and I did not want to waste her time.

However, after three weeks had passed and I felt exactly the same, I decided to pluck up courage and make another appointment. What could I lose! Madam did agree to see me and once again I told her my feelings. This time she listened and said 'well if this is really what you want, I suppose I had better train you'. Practically speechless, I thanked her. Madam then proceeded to tell me what she wanted me to do. The first thing was to watch all the classes she gave at the school. Then I was to watch other teachers taking class and I must also learn the running of the school.

Many years later, when I was driving her home I reminded her of this incident and without any hesitation she said 'I was only testing you, dear!'

By now it was the beginning of February and as I was not earning any money I signed on at the Labour Exchange at Leicester Square, because it seemed to be the one most sympathetic to actors and dancers. I also signed on with an agent, just in case there was some small job that might be suitable.

I well remember my first time of going into the Sadler's Wells School to watch Madam teaching. I took a chair behind the piano, to be well out of everyone's way. When the class came into the centre, Madam called me over to sit with her and from then on she was asking me if I really understood what she was saying and if I could see the difference between the way the students were doing things. There were many classes like this and I soon realised that she was training my eye to see things in the same way that she saw them. When I went into the classes of other teachers, I realised I was looking at them in the way that Madam was teaching me. What a privilege!

Barbara Fewster who had been our ballet mistress on the *Dream* tour, was now on the teaching staff at the school and I was grateful to be to be able to watch her classes.

Within a week of going into the school, I was asked if would like to take part in a television documentary programme called *Dancers of Tomorrow.* It was to be about a girl training at the Sadler's Wells School from the age of ten years until she became a member of the corps de ballet. This was to be produced by Naomi Capon and after an interview, she offered me the part of the senior student going into the corps de ballet.

The programme was scheduled for the 21st of February. Quite a large section of it was filmed in advance, like the classes and the beginning which showed me walking along outside the Opera House, then entering the stage door and walking across and round the stage in amazement at the size of it. The rest of the acting part was live on the night and unfortunately there is no record of that part of the programme.

As it was necessary to keep myself in training, I went to Kathleen Crofton's classes in Great Newport Street, when I had to go to Leicester Square. The Sadler's Wells School said I could do the boys' classes taken by Harold Turner, these were actually of tremendous benefit, because at the same time as I was dancing, I was also learning about teaching boys and the different approach needed.

During this time, I was chosen to be in one of the large dance scenes in the film of *King's Rhapsody*, with Anna Neagle, which gave me a little more work.

Also, I was asked to be the dancer in *Les Sylphides* costume, on the front cover of the Sadler's Wells Theatre Ballet book that year.

The other job that gave me some income, was to model some gloves for *She* magazine. They wanted some one to wear all sorts of different gloves and at the same time show ballet mime gestures, suitable for each type of glove.

The rest of my time was spent at the school watching classes and trying to digest so much information. It really reached a point when I wished to be able to teach and release all this information which was flowing in daily in vast quantities. One day, however, the Director, Arnold Haskell, called me into his office and said they would like to offer me the the position of Junior teacher as from September, with the salary of £2 a week. This was thrilling news! I was so grateful to be asked and I accepted the offer immediately.

At the end of the term and before the summer holidays, there was the two weeks Summer Course for Teachers, which Madam held each year. I was allowed to attend and to sit with all the other members of staff, whose duty it was to be there. Many teachers from all over the country and from abroad were present. The course proved invaluable in deepening and expanding my understanding of Madam's approach to teaching, and for me, it constituted the crowning event of a period in which I had experienced a major change in direction and taken a significant forward step in my evolving career.

Chapter 8

Teaching at the Sadler's Wells School and beginning of the Ballet School at the Koninklijk Conservatorium, Holland

From September 1955 and through the year of 1956 history was being made in the dance world. As I was now a member of the ballet staff at the Sadler's Wells School at Barons Court, I was actually there to be part of it.

Firstly, came the opening of the Sadler's Wells Lower School at White Lodge in Richmond Park. To begin with, there were six boarders from Form 1, and on the 26th of September, Miss McCutcheon, the headmistress, brought them in the Bedford van to Barons Court to join the rest of their class who were day pupils, for their dance classes.

I was there to meet them when they arrived and I really had to laugh to myself, because they looked just as though they had come out of the St Trinians film – all untidy, holding their berets on and loaded with small suitcases and character shoes. They were all chatting away to the others in Form 1 and telling them what wonderful hiding places there were at White Lodge.

At lunch Miss McCutcheon was telling the staff about the various problems she was having with the electric lights and heating. She also mentioned the man who appeared in the front hallway and wanted to see Princess Margaret. He was told to go to Buckingham Palace. Also, she spoke about the deer from the park which had got into the kitchen.

That day marked the beginning of the Benesh Notation. Arnold Haskell, our director, opened with a speech and said that this occasion would go down in history. This was followed by the first lesson given by Rudolf and Joan Benesh. Most of the staff attended, plus Ena Child, one of our pianists, and myself. Afterwards, we had regular lessons throughout that year.

What was so interesting was that on those long train journeys during the Sadler's Wells tour, Joan, who was a member of the company, together with several others, had already been experimenting with this system of notation. It is a way of writing and recording ballets in shorthand, underneath a music stave. In future years, it was to become the Benesh Notation, which is now taught and used throughout the world and most ballet companies have their own choreologist.

That same week, on Friday the 30th, I was held up on the tube train and did not arrive at the school until five to nine, only to be greeted by Barbara Fewster, telling me that I had to teach Form 1 because its regular teacher was off sick. That was to be the first class that I taught at the school and this arrangement continued during the next couple of weeks. I don't think I was overjoyed at taking that class and was glad when their teacher returned.

Saturday the 1st of October marked the beginning of the Junior Associates. These classes were going to be taught by Elizabeth Kennedy. When they arrived, I helped her do the selling of the headbands and belts in their respective colours. Again, this was another piece of history being made, because these classes are now held all over the country and are taught by graduates from the Teachers' Course.

The next day, Sunday, was a great day in the history of White Lodge. All the other boarders arrived and the parents were allowed to wander around the school. The following day all the pupils came in buses to Barons Court, to attend their classical classes. As yet, the studios at White Lodge were not ready for use.

One of the things I had to do in rotation with other members of staff, which none of us really enjoyed, was to take rest duty with all the lower classes after lunch. The children had to collect their rugs from the cupboards in the Baylis Hall and after laying them on the floor, they had to lie down and rest for ten minutes without talking! I don't think they could really understand the reason for this exercise.

The classes were now beginning to be sorted out and several children needed extra coaching to bring them up to the standard of the rest of their class. That was a good opportunity for me to give these extra lessons. I also had a class of seven eleven-year-old boys to teach, which I thoroughly enjoyed. They worked so hard for me. Also, Form 4 and Lower 5 coaching, were a lovely group to teach. Now I was beginning to feel the decision to teach was absolutely right and I was in my right place.

Madam had put me under the direction of Barbara Fewster. However, Winifred Edwards also found things for me to do, like changes to the timetable, which she expected me to type. I could not type, but she showed me the black upright antiquated typewriter in the ballet office and told me to get on with the changes. In those days one would never dream of saying no. It was so hard to press the keys down and of course I had to make carbon copies and change the reel when it ran out. It always seemed that no sooner had I finished her request than Miss Edwards would return and say that it had to be done again, as there were more changes to add.

Remembering the instruction that Madam had given me, that I must learn about the running of the school, I felt I was certainly learning about timetables and tried to be alert to all that was going on around me. As the school had now acquired the use of number 46 Colet Gardens next door, I was always being sent on errands throughout both buildings. In those days there were no intercom telephones. It always had to be a runner and that happened to be me. Arnold Haskell said I needed roller skates!

My days were really full from the moment I arrived before 9 a.m. until after 6.30 p.m. and often later when we had auditions. My £2 a week was not going very far and I bought a bicycle for £3 from a friend, hoping to ride the five miles to the school and then back again, in order to save the tube fares. However, I found it was all too much.

By March of the following year I had spent all my savings from the two American tours and sadly realised that I would have to leave and get another job which would pay more. I went to see Mr Haskell to explain my position and told him that I only had enough money to see me through that week. He left me and went to see the bursar. When he returned, he had the wonderful news that from then on I would receive £5 a week! I could manage on that, as I was living at home.

Sometime during 1954 Arnold Haskell and Kurt Jooss from Germany visited Holland at the invitation of the Netherlands Government Commission. This consisted of Sonia Gaskell and other prominent people from the ballet scene in Holland. Their purpose was to consider and report on the formation of a Netherlands Ballet Company. Soon it was agreed that Sonia Gaskell's group should receive this official recognition and that their base would be in The Hague.

There were also two other groups at this time. The Ballet of the Low Countries, directed by Mascha ter Weeme, and the Scapino group, which specialised in children's programmes and visited schools.

The all important need now, was to have a school with a full ballet curriculum, to be able to supply the three companies with dancers. A request from the Netherlands Government Commission was then made to the Sadler's Wells School, asking if one of their teachers could go to Holland and form a school at the Koninklijk Conservatorium voor Muziek at The Hague.

This is when I came into the picture. Arnold Haskell called me into his office one day and asked if I would be interested in going to Holland to run this Ballet School. It seemed to me to be a wonderful opportunity (although at the time, I did not really realise what would be involved). An interview was arranged at his house in Chelsea, on Friday the 27th of July 1956, with Sonia Gaskell and Everhard van Beijnum, the under director of the Koninklijk Conservatorium.

This was a day and experience I shall never forget. They tried to explain about the Koninklijk Conservatorium and that they had had ballet classes there, also, that it was a very old building. They were very keen to stress and show me the plans and drawings for the ballet studios in the beautiful new building, which would be ready in three years time. They said that I would have every thing I needed, including a theatre. (Little did they know that it would take another twenty years after I left for it all to come to fruition.) My brief was to train dancers for the three ballet companies.

The interview seemed to go well, although I believe they thought I was rather young, but Arnold Haskell was able to assure them that I had all the necessary knowledge, discipline and qualities they needed. Just over a week later, I received a letter from Mr van Beijnum, to say that I had been appointed as a teacher of dancing at the Koninklijk Conservatorium. However, he now had to receive the blessing of this appointment from the Minister of Education, Arts and Sciences.

This interview had taken place at the end of the first week of the two weeks summer course given by Madam. It was again a very inspiring time for me. One of the things she stressed was 'to be light, one had to think lightly,' and that speed was impossible if one was not light. Also, she gave one of her Irish statements – 'keep off your toes, when you are on them!'

Before the term finished on Saturday the 4th of August, the staff gave me a Harrod's gift voucher for £5, which I was so grateful for because it enabled me to buy new buttons and a belt for my winter coat and other things which I needed. When I said 'good-bye' to Madam, her last words to me were. ' Go and get on with it dear, it will be good for you.' Little did she or I know what lay ahead of me.

By the 24th of August I heard that my appointment had been approved and I could now go ahead and get a loan from the bank in order to purchase my air ticket. My grandmother, who was living with us at the time, suggested that I might like my mother to accompany me for the first week and that she would pay for her expenses. What a wonderful gesture that was and I was absolutely thrilled. Before leaving we were given three introductions to look up when we arrived, which we appreciated very much.

* * *

On Sunday the 2nd of September we flew to Schipol Airport, in Amsterdam. It was my mother's first flight, so that was a new experience for her and to be one of many to follow. We then caught a KLM bus to The Hague, where we took a taxi to the hotel where we had been booked for a week. They immediately asked for our passports and said they would be returned to us when we left the hotel. That gave me a very strange feeling for starters, but gradually I had to learn that they had been an occupied country and it was only ten years since the end of the war, and their approach to things was certainly different from what I was used to.

The next day I walked to the Koninklijk Conservatorium which was about ten minutes away from the hotel, right in the centre of The Hague. I had not been given a time to arrive, but decided 10 a.m. would probably be suitable. I was greeted by the caretaker, who did not speak English, and he called for Mr van Beijnum. When in London, I had found him to be very pleasant and reassuring, so I was immediately made to feel at ease.

We then walked down the corridor. At the end there were two doors, the one on the right was for percussion instrument lessons and the one on the left was the ballet studio. My first impression was that it was very small. Two runs and a *jeté* and two more runs, and that would be the length of a diagonal line. How could I possibly train dancers for the company in that small space! Then there was the question of the 'kackel', a coal fire which took up space on one side. I was introduced to Mr van Duuren the pianist, who fortunately spoke English. He had been chosen for me and was standing by a beautiful new baby grand piano. On the same side there were a few steps down to a small room, which was to be the changing room. Unfortunately, the only way to get to it was through the studio.

At this point my feelings about the place were already becoming uneasy and then I asked Mr van Beijnum the all important question, 'How many pupils do you have?' The reply came back, 'We don't have any Miss Adams, what would you like us to do about it?' After a pause, I said, 'you had better put an advertisement in the paper tonight, stating that we will be holding an audition this Wednesday the 5th of September at 4 p.m.'

Mr van Beijnum then showed me over the rest of the building and when we reached the concert hall I asked if perhaps sometimes it could be used for a ballet studio. 'Oh no', he said, 'there are fire regulations that do not permit us moving the seating.' But he said, 'when we have the new building, you will have all the space you need.' What a long wait that turned out to be!

While there I was given my contract in English, which I had asked for in advance, and the administrator kindly went through it with me. When it came to the holidays, I insisted that I should have the ones of the Koninklijk Conservatorium, especially in July and August. This would then enable me to go to the Sadler's Wells School and watch classes and attend Madam's summer course, in order to keep up with the work going on there. I was also given medical papers, all in Dutch, which had to be filled in before having a medical. The administrator also went through all these with me.

I then went back to the hotel. Was I glad to have my mother there, to be able to discuss all that had gone on during that morning. I really felt that, had she not been there, I would have been on the first flight home. Earlier that day, I had contacted one of the friends to whom I had been given an introduction and she invited us to tea that afternoon.

This friend, Gratia, lived with her family in Wassenaar, about a twenty-minute tram ride outside The Hague. The trams were old-fashioned ones in comparison to the ones we had seen earlier in the town and we had an interesting ride out into the countryside. When we reached our destination, we had to walk down a couple of lanes until we reached her home, a lovely large thatched house. We were greeted very warmly and I immediately began to feel a little better about the whole situation.

Fortunately, I had brought my contract and medical papers with me, so that I could check them through again with Gratia, who spoke excellent English. What a blessing that was, because all the medical questions had been answered incorrectly. We had a thoroughly enjoyable time and were invited to go again the following Sunday.

The next day, Tuesday, I had to report to The Hague Police, as a foreign person working in Holland. That really was a scary experience. When I entered the room, it was filled with cigar smoke, and the Police Inspector asked in a very rough way 'why are you in Holland?' I, of course, thought he must already know. He was so unpleasant and made me feel as though I was a criminal, and not someone who was there to help them with a Ballet School.

The following day the first audition took place and Sonia Gaskell came to be with me. I don't remember how many turned up, but we chose fifteen to start with and this included one boy. Their ages ranged between nine and twenty-one, and they were divided into three classes. The classes would commence the following week on Monday the 10th of September.

Sonia Gaskell said to me that as I had nothing to do for the rest of the week, she would like me to take the Netherlands Ballet Company class the following day. Another challenge to face, having never taken a company class before. As it turned out, it seemed to go extremely well, but I must say, as I walked in and saw that all the company, plus soloists were there, I hoped that the class I had prepared in my mind was going to be suitable. However, the moment one is able to start helping people to do things better, they are open to learning and that is when everything starts to come together, and I enjoyed it too.

On the Saturday, I had to go to the hospital for the medical taking with me the forms which had now been correctly filled in. Everything was fine, so that was good.

While my mother was still with me, we did some sight-seeing and began to try and make ourselves familiar with our surroundings. The following day, Sunday, we had another visit to the friends in Wassenaar. This time they came up with a wonderful suggestion of where I could live for the time being. This was something we had discussed on our previous visit, and after we had left, the four children had asked Gratia if I could stay in their house with them. Apparently they had all agreed that if I was happy to do that, they would be pleased. The arrangement was that I would be there as a paying guest. As far as I was concerned, it was a good temporary arrangement until I really felt happy to go it alone. I think my mother was relieved as well.

Monday the 10th of September was the beginning of the Ballet School at the Koninklijk Conservatorium, and the first class took place at 9.30 a.m. until 11 a.m. followed by the second class, and after lunch the third class finished at 3 p.m. At the beginning, the classes seemed to take place at different times each day, until everything was sorted out. The first Dutch word I learnt was to turn round, so that helped when the children were at the barre and needed to turn to the other side.

Mr Pierhagen had been appointed headmaster, but could not take up his post until January. In the meantime Mrs Prinsen-Geerlings, who was also one of the educational team, was taking his place. Besides their education, the pupils also had to learn a musical instrument and attend Dalcroze Eurhythmic classes, given by Maria van der Heijde. This was also taught to pupils at the Sadler's Wells School by Desiree Martin. The interesting thing was that both these teachers had studied together in Switzerland.

As soon as the term started, I searched around to find a suitable uniform for the pupils – black leotards, pink tights or pink socks for the younger ones. I was able to find a shop in The Hague that stocked Freed's ballet shoes, so that was convenient. I also wanted each class to have its own colour of headband and belt. When Mr van Beijnum heard about this, I was told in no uncertain terms that I could not enforce a uniform, because only children from a reform school wore a uniform! My reply was, 'all the corps de ballet in *Swan Lake* wear the same costume'. Happily that was the end of the problem and all the pupils were happy too.

This same day, my mother and I visited some more friends and they offered to put us up until my mother left on the following Thursday. This worked out very well, because they were able to take us to Amsterdam and show us all the sights there, before my time was totally filled with work.

On Friday the 14th I held another audition and accepted a few more pupils. I took only those that I felt possibly had enough talent to enter the company, but there did not seem to be much real talent around.

On the 19th I moved to Wassenaar and soon began to feel more settled. I had a small room at the top of the house under the thatched roof, but it was adequate for my needs and had a lovely view over the back garden. After the tram ride, and walking down the lanes in the dark, I needed a torch, as there was only the occasional light.

Before long I had to go and register with the police there. What a difference from before, they were so pleasant. From then on, every time I left the country and returned, I had to report to the police.

We had our first press conference on the 4th of October, with *Haagsche Courant* and also with a magazine called *Eva*. They followed Ingrid Polak, at nine years old she was the youngest pupil we had accepted, through a day at the school, taking pictures of her in all her classes.

The conditions at the Koninklijk Conservatorium were less than ideal and we had to put up with many discomforts. I mentioned earlier about the changing room being situated just off the studio. It never seemed possible for all of a class to come in or go out at the same time. So there was a constant flow of pupils, and as the studio was so small, it was a disruption. The 'kachel', the coal fire, was a problem when Mr Fakkel, the caretaker, would fill it with coke just before 9 a.m. and the studio was full of smoke when we started class. That was the only form of heating in the building. The other disturbance was from the room next door, where they were giving percussion lessons. I would be in the middle of arranging an Adage when suddenly there would be a crash of cymbals or the beating of drums.

I had to get used to pupils asking for the day off when someone in the family had a birthday. Sometimes I would win by telling them how much they would be missing, but at other times, the parents would call and say their child must be free. During the cold weather, it was not unusual to receive a message from Mr Pierhagen to say the school would be finishing early, because the tennis courts had been frozen over to allow skating. I had to learn a lot about the Dutch ways and customs!

More auditions were held on the 13th and 30th of October and the

8th of December, and each time we accepted a few more students. On the 10th, before the Christmas holidays, I had appointments with the parents to discuss the progress that had been made.

During this first term, I had said to Mr van Beijnum that in the future I would like to have the Royal Academy of Dancing examinations. However, he did not agree and said that the dance students must take examinations of the Koninklijk Conservatorium and that I should have them prepared for the following June. Another new experience!

The Christmas holidays had now arrived and I was certainly looking forward to being at home after that very eventful first term in Holland.

In London there was still some of the term left before the Sadler's Wells School closed for Christmas, which gave me the opportunity to watch classes. It was so good to see them again and realise what a long way we had to go in Holland before attaining the standard required. It was lovely, too, to be at home again and to see my little dog and be able to relax from what had been an amazing experience, living in a country with a different language and not really understanding all that was going on.

On the 10th of January I returned to Holland to start the new term. It was now necessary to incorporate extra classes for Class 3, the senior ones, such as Pointe Work, Solo Dances and Mime. Also, I needed to give private tuition to the one fifteen-year-old boy. This meant that I was now teaching six to seven hours on Mondays, Tuesdays, Thursdays and Fridays, four hours on Wednesdays, and three hours on Saturdays, besides running the school. I was also taking company class three times a month. Things were all beginning to be too much.

Another audition was held on the 19th of January and this time Sonia Gaskell turned up, bringing with her Olga de Haas, whom she had been teaching in Amsterdam. She was twelve and certainly had more of the talent I was looking for. In fact, in later years, she was to become the leading ballerina of the company. So I was very grateful that Sonia Gaskell felt that she could trust me with her further training.

On the 4th of March the friends with whom I was living moved house. However, they were happy that I should stay with them, as they had a guest room. It was a beautiful modern L-shaped house, with a lovely garden and nearer to the tram stop than before. I had a lovely room with large bed and its own miniature bathroom in a cupboard.

Living with this family had certainly been a great help to me during that first term, knowing that I always had someone to turn to if there was a need. The four children naturally wanted to speak English. However, some Dutch was beginning to filter through and at that point, I would have liked to have some lessons. However, more demands were now going to come my way.

Sadly on the 10th of March Mr van Beijnum passed on. He loved the ballet and was a very strong supporter of the Ballet School. For me, things were never the same after that, because I felt I was dealing with people who did not have the same interest in wanting the Ballet School to succeed. It was sad, too, because he missed our first public performance which was to come in just a few weeks' time.

There was another surprise around the corner, when a message came through from Sonia Gaskell that I was to prepare the children for a public performance on the 25th of March at the Koninklijk Schouwburg. It would be called *Van Petit Rat Tot Solist*, and the children, now twenty-nine girls, and three boys, would open the programme by showing class work. Then the Netherlands Ballet Company would provide the rest of it. I then had to set to and prepare the presentation. As I had not prepared anything like this before, I just had to trust that what I had prepared was acceptable. Fortunately, everything did go smoothly and the children did their very best and the press reviews were good.

I had asked my mother to fly over for support and the family agreed that she too could stay in the house and be in my room. I needed her to help me with the make-up of the children.

From the 1st of April, the week after the performance, seemed a good time to regroup the pupils into four classes, and when possible to give the three boys a lesson on their own. Length of classes had to be shortened slightly, but this did not matter now that the ages were better arranged. The term finished on the 16th of April.

It was while I was in London over Easter that I heard the news that the Sadler's Wells Ballet Companies would now be known as The Royal Ballet and the school would be called The Royal Ballet School.

The summer term started on the 29th of April. Just occasionally, it was possible to take the senior class to the company studio in the Koningstraat, when they were away. This gave the students more room to move, and I really had to concentrate on Allegro steps and teaching them to cover the ground.

During the past two terms I had been holding auditions whenever anyone applied, because I did not want to miss out on any talent. Our aim was to get the number up to fifty.

Near the end of the term, I heard the most wonderful news: that one of the senior students had been accepted into the Netherlands Ballet Company. I knew then that the Ballet School had begun to fulfil its purpose of feeding the company with dancers.

1951. With my two dancing
teachers in Bournemouth,
left, Ida Stewart and right,
Elizabeth Collins

1951. After receiving RAD
Solo Seal. Tutu made of paint-
straining muslin.
Photo: Crescent Studios,
Boscombe.

1952. The author with Russell Kerr in costume for the opera *A Masked Ball*.

1953. *Swan Lake* at the Royal Opera House, dance of the six princesses.

1953. The author, photographed by Maurice Seymour in New York.

1953. The author, photographed by Maurice Seymour in New York.

Left.
1953. Sadler's Wells ballet tour of USA and Canada. I took this photo of Margot Fonteyn being lifted by Leslie Edwards during one of the train stops to cool down the engines.

Lower left.
1954. Margot Fonteyn in clogs taken on the ferry after the tour of Holland.

Lower right.
1954. Poster outside the stage door at the Metropolitan Opera House.

1961. Senior students from the Ballet School at the Koninklijk Conservatorium dancing the Garland Dance from *Sleeping Beauty.*

1972. My parents together again after my father had retired from the sea.

1977. Hope Keelan, my assistant, being given away by my father at her wedding.

1984. Left to right, Barbara Fewster, Michael Wood, myself and Graham Bowles, the day of his retirement at White Lodge.

1988. A lovely picture of 'Madam' celebrating her 90th birthday, taken on Diploma Day. Photo: Mike Martin.

1988. Also on that day, the author with 'Madam'.

Upper left.
1988. On the left Julia Ellis, who had
been my assistant for two years,
handing over to Caroline Barrett.

Upper right.
1990. Dimitra Kouremeti my assistant
on right, handing over to Clare
Howarth.

Lower left.
1991. Clare handing over to Teresa
Hallam who stayed with me for two
years.

1991. My dear mother who had such an
eye for colour, line and design.

1991. Snoopy doing his duty on the last day of term before Christmas.

1993. With Danella Bedford, my last assistant. Photo: Mike Martin.

1995. At my retirement with Thomas McLelland Young, the pianist who helped me so much over the years.

1995. The final ceremony. 'This is your life' together with 'Madam', Dame Merle, my mother. Photo: Mike Martin.

Chapter 9

Continuing with my adventure in Holland

Just a few days before the end of the summer term I received a message from Sonia Gaskell that she would like me to take company classes during the month of July. What a blessing that I had insisted on having the Koninklijk Conservatorium holidays incorporated into my contract! Otherwise, I would not have been able to watch the classes at The Royal Ballet School or attend Madam's summer course.

The holidays for me were always a happy time and seemed to pass so quickly. Little did I know that when I returned to Holland at the end of August, besides the wonderful news that two more of the senior students had been accepted into the company, one joining as a soloist, I would be presented with yet another challenge.

The term started on the 2nd of September 1957 and I soon realised that it was again necessary to regroup the classes because of increasing numbers. From now on there would be five classes.

During the summer holidays one of the senior students had put on a lot of weight and I could see that although she was technically very capable, she would not be suitable for entry into any of the three ballet companies. So I spoke to Mr Geraedts, who had replaced Mr van Beijnum on a temporary basis, and explained the situation. He said he would write to the parents. The reply came back that their daughter was not with us to be a dancer, but a teacher. They ran one of the largest dance schools in Rotterdam and one day expected their daughter to take over the school. Then Mr Geraedts just looked at me and said, 'you will need to run a teachers course in your programme'. My time was already full, but now I had to work evenings as well to prepare for this course.

At that time there were no technical books on ballet in Holland, so I called home for my books to be sent to me. I then started to write papers on all the exercises at the barre, and in the centre, in fact everything I could possible find out, to be able to help the students. I asked all the other senior students if they would be interested in also doing these classes, and seven of them agreed to attend. My mother used to say, 'if you really know the reason why, and how, you will do it so much better'. So this course could only be of benefit to all the students attending. The first lesson took place on Thursday the 10th of October and I was just one lesson ahead of the class each week. The interesting thing about these technical theory notes is that they were to be used throughout my teaching career.

On the 28th of November there was to be a public opera performance given at the Koninklijk Conservatorium. Mr Geraedts asked me to arrange two Minuet pieces, for *Thésée* (1675), and the *Ballet Furiendans for Iphigenie en Tauride* (1778). For these dances, I would be using students from the senior class. To fit the necessary rehearsals into an already busy timetable presented a problem.

During this time, to keep everything running as smoothly as possible, I decided to ask three of the students taking the Teachers' Course to help me with the teaching of the two lower classes. I felt confident enough to leave them to teach these classes, just as a temporary measure, until the opera performance was over. It seemed to work extremely well and gave the girls some teaching experience. I had been asking for an assistant for some time, but this seemed to be of no avail.

Before the term finished for the Christmas break, there was good news once again in that another one of the senior students was taken into the company.

In January 1958, Mr Kees van Baaren became the overall Director of the Koninklijk Conservatorium. Unfortunately he did not have any knowledge of ballet.

Arrangements had now been made for us to have the use of a gymnasium, attached to a school in the Korte Lombardstraat. This was five minutes walk from the main building. There was no telephone for many months and when a call came through for me from the Minister of Arts, a runner would be sent from the Conservatorium. I was expected to stop teaching and run over the cobble stones to take the call.

There was one occasion, when my mother was visiting and watching the class I was taking, when this happened. This time I asked her to continue with the class. She had never done anything like that before, but obviously made a good impression, because one of the children came to me afterwards and said, 'is your mother a teacher, because she gave us corrections?' My mother had learnt a lot from watching my classes when I was training! As much as I tried to have this arrangement improved, because it was the Minister of Arts, that was the way it had to be.

The only real advantage of this gymnasium was that it did give us more space, but the shape was not really what was required. We had to use the gymnastic rails for barres, except for a short barre in front of a mirror, which we had to lock up behind shutters. Conditions were not good with regard to the changing rooms and there was no running water. When I asked the Ministry of Arts for some water for the children to wash their feet, they provided what I called a 'pigs trough', a stone sink, close to the ground, with only cold water. About a year later, the educational classes also moved into this same building. However, the slight improvements then made did not affect the dancers. There were no showers in the changing rooms all the time I was there.

I had now received the date for our annual performance, which was to be on Monday the 28th of April. This time I was asked to fill the whole of the first half of the programme before the interval and then the Netherlands Ballet Company would complete the second half.

I arranged that Class 1 would show exercises at the Barre. Class 2 would show exercises in the Centre; Class 3 at the Barre; Class 4 Adage at the Barre and then *enchaînements* in the Centre. Class 5 would then show an Adage in the Centre followed by *enchaînements*. The one boy in Class 5 would dance a solo, and the senior girls would dance the 'Morning Hours' from the ballet *Coppélia*.

This time, I needed help with the make-up for the children, as there were now many more of them. One of the education teachers put on the base, I did the eyes, and my mother, who had come over for the performance, with a steady hand did the lips. Quite a picture seeing all those children, lined up for this tricky operation.

Again I was left to arrange everything, and once more had to trust that what I had prepared was suitable for the occasion, and would meet the approval of Sonia Gaskell. Fortunately the two newspapers *Het Vaderland* and *Haagsche Courant*, were most encouraging and pleased with what they had seen. However, after all the work that had taken place, I was now seriously considering my position and wondering if it was really worth staying.

We now had to prepare for the examinations in June. If we had any doubt about the progress of any of the children or students, we always discussed this with the parents before going on holiday at Easter. They were then prepared, should the examinations prove to be unsatisfactory. As the Ballet School was subsidised by the government, the parents only paid a token fee, and we were obliged to keep only those that were making good progress.

At the end of the term, there was more good news when another three of the senior students were accepted into the Netherlands Ballet Company. That meant that seven had been accepted during the first two years. I really was happy about this, because it meant that the Ballet School was doing what it was there for and that I must be doing something right.

The joy for me during the month of July was always in going back to The Royal Ballet School. Watching classes and seeing the standard required was an inspiration, and in my mind, I felt I must always be prepared in case Madam should ever pay us a visit in Holland.

While there I had talks with Madam and Arnold Haskell, who were both very pleased to hear how well things were progressing, and he said that I was making history! However, I was less concerned with history than with gaining some much needed assistance.

In September 1958, I returned to Holland, and as there was no assistance in sight, I decided to have the help of one of the three senior students, who had done so previously. She had taught very well before and I felt I could trust her to do a good job. This was on an unofficial basis and only when she was free to do so. Everything now seemed to be well established and running to plan.

In the new year I left the family in Wassenaar and took a bed sitting room in The Hague. It was on the first floor of a house conveniently situated, just off the number 9 tram route. I had searched for a flat, but either the travelling was not suitable, or they were too expensive. I always had to remember that I wanted to return to London for the holidays, and that for me, being in Holland was really only a temporary arrangement.

On Monday the 9th of February our students were invited to join in with a youth programme at the Koninklijk Schouwburg theatre. Using the students from Classes 4 and 5, they danced the Peasant Dance, from the ballet *Giselle*, Act I. This had taken quite a considerable number of rehearsals but they seemed to rise to the challenge very well.

After having the examinations in June, we had a visit from Lord Wakehurst, Governor of Northern Ireland. He was also a Governor of The Royal Ballet. He was visiting Holland to attend the Jubilee Celebrations of the Dutch Order of St John. He wanted to talk with me about the Ballet School and to see the children in class. He also wanted to meet Dr Hulska, the Minister of Arts, and Mr van Baaren. Besides all this, he would like to watch a rehearsal of the Netherlands Ballet Company, all in a couple of days!

What a job that was to arrange! However, it was all sorted out and I had dinner with him after he arrived at his hotel on Wednesday the 17th of June.

Prior to the visit of Lord Wakehurst to the school, I had to train the children, who would be in their education classes at the time, to be able to stand up behind their desks when he entered the room. This was something they were not used to doing and it took quite some time to accomplish. The fashion then was to wear very full skirts and as they stood up, the skirts knocked the chairs over.

On the day everything went very smoothly up to the last moment when I opened the door for Lord Wakehurst to leave. I remember Mary, the smallest pupil rushing through the open door under my arm. We were both speechless, but had a good laugh about it! The visit had been very successful, and by what I could gather, he had obviously given a good report on his return to London.

During my summer break in 1959, I made an appointment to see Madam. I was now beginning to feel that the school in Holland was thoroughly established and ready to be handed over to someone else. I really felt I had given my all to the Ballet School and would like to return to London. Madam said, that she had no place in London, but would very much like it if I would be interested in going to run her school in Ankara, Turkey. This seemed an inviting prospect and I said I would be interested. She said she would make all the arrangements with the director, however, I should not give in my notice in Holland until I received the contract.

When returning to Holland in September 1959, I found to my amazement that Sonia Gaskell had arranged for me to have an assistant. It turned out to be one of my students but not the one who had been helping me throughout the previous year. How could this have been done without knowing anything about the work of the student? I told Mr van Baaren that I was not happy with the arrangement or with the fact that I had not been consulted, but he said it had already been settled and could not be altered. This again was something making me feel very uneasy about the situation. However, I had to press on regardless.

This same month, the State Examinations for Dance came into operation in Holland, but the Koninklijk Conservatorium decided not to participate. The standard required for them was very low and it was decided to continue with our own, which were now well established. I revised the syllabus for all our classes because our standard had now risen to be on a par with the Royal Academy of Dancing, in London. We were now also giving a Teaching Certificate.

This term we also introduced Historical Dance classes into the programme for the senior students and these classes were given by Mr Schultink, an expert in this field of dance.

Sonia Gaskell was away in Paris during the whole of this year and the company was being run by Benjamin Harkarvy in her absence. This meant that we did not have to prepare for a performance.

In February 1960 my contract came through to go to Ankara. When I looked at it, I realised I could not accept. For some time, I had been having difficulty eating the Dutch food – how could I possibly manage the Turkish food? However, if I did not accept, I felt that Madam would probably not speak to me again. I telephoned my mother and explained the situation. She just said, 'you should never make a decision on fear'. I then knew quite clearly that I was hesitating to say I could not accept the contract because I was afraid of Madam's reaction. How wrong I was to think that, because I was about to experience the other side of Madam, which I have already mentioned earlier.

I sent Madam a cable to explain the situation, saying that I was very sorry not to be able to go through with the contract. Her reply to me was amazing. She said it was rather a shock, but she had been partly expecting it, as she thought the director in Ankara was greatly at fault in holding up his final acceptance for so long. She continued, 'in all fairness to you, I do feel that you were living far too long in the state of indecision, resulting in your present position. In many ways, I must say, I am sorry.' She also said in her own handwriting, that she would deal with it all. What a letter to receive from Madam. That just proved that she could be very considerate and understanding. Many years later she said to me, 'it would never have been right for you to go to Turkey.' How wonderful the way things do work out.

The auditions now were mainly for the new intake into Class 1, and as time passed we were able to become more selective.

By now I had heard of a flat a little further down the road on the other side. On the first floor there was the kitchen and sitting room, which had a small balcony over looking the garden, and on the second floor was the bedroom and bathroom. It certainly gave me more space than before and I could invite people to see me, although the furniture was rather sparse.

Earlier in the year I asked Mr van Baaren if they would pay for my assistant to go to London and attend Madam's summer course at The Royal Ballet School, as I felt this would be of great benefit to her. Fortunately, they agreed.

Returning in September 1960 after the summer holiday, at the beginning of my fifth year, the first thing I decided to do was to change the name of Classes 4 and 5 to Senior I and Senior II. Also, those students nearing graduation into the company, would be called Theatre Class.

This year Sonia Gaskell had engaged Mr Kumusnikov from the Kirov Company to be Ballet Master of the Netherlands Ballet. I felt this was a wonderful opportunity to try and have him teach our senior students on a Saturday morning and I would also be able to watch his classes. This was agreed and proved to be so helpful.

Around Christmas time I really decided that this would be my last year. So during the spring term I spoke to Mr van Baaren about my decision. He seemed to find it difficult to understand why I should want to leave such a good position. I did realise what a privilege it was to work at the Koninklijk Conservatorium, but it had never been my intention to stay there all my working days, as I always hoped to be able to return to The Royal Ballet School. I told him that I would be writing to Dame Ninette de Valois and Arnold Haskell, with the view that they might have some suggestions about a replacement for me.

During my Easter break in London, I spoke to several people about the position at the Koninklijk Conservatorium, but no one seemed interested in leaving London. It was not an easy place to fill, because it needed someone with theatre experience who could also run a school. When making enquiries it seemed to be difficult to find someone with the right qualifications and experience in both these fields.

On my return to Holland, I handed in my official resignation letter to Mr van Baaren and explained that I had been trying to find a replacement for the position, but that he now needed to take over the job of finding someone for September.

Monday the 12th of June at Het Gebouw voor Kunsten and Wetenschappen was the date and place where our next performance was to be held. This theatre was larger than the one we had previously used. Again, it was to take up the whole of the first half of the programme and be called 'Van Petit Rat Tot Solist.'

I now needed to start preparing for this and wanted to be able to show more dances from the classical repertoire, after the Class Work.

We started with Class 2 at the Barre, then Class 3 doing Centre Work, Senior I, would show Centre Work. Senior II and Theatre Class would also show work in the Centre, which included *Porte de Bras, Adage,* one of the boys working alone, and an *Entrée* and *Allegro Enchaînements.* Then the Senior students showed some of the Historical Dances they had learnt with Mr Schultink.

Following that, all the Classes showed Dances. Then, Senior II and Theatre Class danced the Garland Dance from the ballet *Sleeping Beauty.* After that we continued with solos: Aurora's Variation, from Act I, then the Fairy of The Crystal Fountain, The Garden Fairy, The Songbird Fairy, Fairy of The Woodland Glade from the Prologue, and the girls Blue Bird Variation, from Act III. The two senior boys did a Variation together, and then it all finished with a Grand Finale.

It certainly was an achievement that we now had students capable of performing these solos in public, and something I was especially pleased about, considering it was to be my last performance with them. The reviews in the newspapers were very good and proved that the Ballet School was well established and providing the dancers needed for the company. Those graduating that year were of a very good standard and later this was proved when most of them became soloists in the Netherlands Ballet.

I now felt happy to leave, knowing that everything was running well and completely under control. In fact, any teacher with the right qualifications and experience could just go in and take over. The big question was, who? I kept asking Mr van Baaren if they had had any success with their enquiries, but the answer was always, no. My assistant was also leaving to get married.

On my last evening a farewell dinner had been arranged by the

Koninklijk Conservatorium, at the Corona Hotel. Twelve of my closest colleagues were there, which was a pleasant surprise, and that gave me the opportunity to thank them for all their kindness and hospitality while I was in their country.

Being in Holland had been an amazing experience and not only at the Koninklijk Conservatorium. To meet so many kind people who had been through such a traumatic time, during the occupation of their country in World War II, was humbling to say the least. I had been warned by the staff to treat those children born in 1944 very carefully, because their parents had probably been living on bulbs at the time. Some of my friends had actually shown me the stove where they had roasted the bulbs. I had been told numerous stories from friends about the problems they went through and it only made me more grateful.

Before leaving I was given a photograph album filled with lots of photographs of the pupils in school at the last rehearsal before the performance, and at the performance. It was a lovely reminder of all the friends I had made.

Because of having so much luggage, I had to make my last journey home by ferry, and the following day, a further surprise awaited me at The Hook of Holland. There, to see me off, were a number of the staff, parents and pupils. What a touching gesture that was. I was so grateful to have Hanneke Berlage, one of my senior students, travelling with me. She was going to stay with me for a week and watch classes in London. Without her with me I think I would have found it difficult saying goodbye. And together with the sadness at parting with so many dear friends, I could not help wondering how the school would resolve the problem of my replacement in time for its re-opening in September.

Chapter 10

Returning to London and The Royal Ballet School

Just four days after returning to London for the holidays I received a telephone call from Mr van Baaren, asking if I already had a job to go to, and if not, would I reconsider going back to the Ballet School at the Koninklijk Conservatorium. To the first question, I replied, 'no, not yet.' Then all of a sudden, those five years of extremely hard work establishing the Ballet School just seemed to flash past in front of my eyes and I found myself saying that I would return until Christmas, to give them more time to find another teacher. When I went downstairs to tell my mother, she just could not believe what I had said. She knew how much I wanted to return to London. However, I assured her that I would be back home in time for Christmas.

Soon after making this decision, I contacted the friends with whom I had been living originally, and they said that they would be happy for me to stay with them again.

Having Hanneke with me for that week was lovely and we were able to watch classes at The Royal Ballet School and discuss a number of things together. I asked her if she would like to help me when we returned to Holland and she was thrilled.

So when I returned to the Koninklijk Conservatorium I asked for Hanneke to be my assistant. This was granted, unlike a number of others things which I had asked for previously, and had been refused. One of these was the Royal Academy of Dancing Examinations. I felt so strongly that examiners outside the Ballet School should be examining the students.

Since being in Holland, I had tried to attend as many ballet performances of the company as I could, but now it was much more interesting watching those who had been at the Ballet School and seeing the progress they were making. With the last intake there were now at least ten, possibly twelve. The only thing that concerned me was that I felt some of them were being asked to dance roles before they were really ready for them.

It was now important to prepare for the RAD examinations, which would be held in January. I asked Mr van Baaren if I could have Maud Kool, the RAD representative in Holland, to come and give some classes, as she would be absolutely up to date with the work. She apparently said that I was quite capable of doing it. However, I needed her to see the students and check that the work was accurate. Also, the boys' syllabus had been changed at the last Assembly, which I had not attended. This meant that I needed to go to Maud Kool's studio in Haarlem and learn the boys' syllabus. While there, I asked if she could teach the students after I had left, for the week or so prior to the examinations in January. She said she had not been told that I was leaving – Mr van Baaren had only mentioned that I was just thinking about it. Mr Pierhagen also said I could not leave, because everything was running so well. Hearing those remarks really gave me a clear picture of what was going on and I knew what I had to do.

A couple of weeks before it was time for me to leave, the students were looking good in preparation for their RAD examinations. I felt that the two boys entering were doing extremely well with the Elementary and Intermediate, and if they had a good result for the first exam, they could also take the second (this was allowed when taking the exams abroad). Hanneke too, was taking the Intermediate, and I knew she was capable of teaching the classes in January if Maud Kool was unable to. I felt awful about leaving them to get on with it, but I could now see quite clearly that there was only one solution to this problem and that was to leave.

When saying goodbye to everyone, it just seemed so strange because they kept saying, 'see you in January,' and when I said 'no,' they just said, 'you left once and came back and that is what will happen again.' So I just slipped away quietly.

One of the memories I still have to this day, was of the summer time, walking to and from the Koninklijk Conservatorium, situated in the Korte Beestenmarkt. This was a very short road, and because they had not had enough space for many years, they rented rooms in the houses opposite. When it was warm and the windows were open, one could hear this amazing sound of all sorts of instruments being played, and it gave the place such an atmosphere.

In January, when I did not return and there was no replacement for me, Hanneke and Maud Kool held the fort and saw that the examinations were conducted smoothly. The results were good and the two boys, as I expected, received Honours for both their Elementary and Intermediate examinations. This turned out to be the last and only time that RAD examinations were held at the Koninklijk Conservatorium. However, later you will read how having these examinations was all part of the jigsaw that went to make up my career.

Before long Mr Witaly Osins arrived from the Bolshoi Academy in Moscow to take over the running of the Ballet School and Hanneke joined the company.

* * *

How wonderful it was to be home, but I was so grateful to have had that amazing and challenging experience in Holland, however tough it had seemed to be. I certainly would never have accepted the position had I known that they really expected me to stay until I retired. As far as I was concerned, I had completed the job that I was asked to do.

My mother was now living alone with our dog as my father was at sea in the Far East and only came ashore when the ship was in for a re-fit. My grandmother, who had been so wonderful to us, had passed on in New Zealand. My mother and I had always been happy together, so it was only natural to want to be at home with her.

Soon after Christmas, I made an appointment to see Madam and to ask her if she had any place for me in London. She said 'she was not expecting any changes to take place to the staff', and suggested that I look elsewhere.

I then attended the RAD Special Week and spoke to a number of teachers there. One was Mrs Grandison-Clark, who owned the Grandison College in East Croydon, and she offered me two days a week of teaching there, which I accepted. Joan Lawson was also teaching there at the same time. On one day I was required to take eight half hour private lessons and two classes. The other day was six half hour private lessons and three classes. All these lessons were of the RAD syllabus. The private lessons took place in the garage and the heating was minimal. As it was winter time I had to keep my coat on all the time. I felt so sorry for the students who were obliged to wear their dancing uniform.

It was all good experience working in a different type of school which was training students for the musical theatre. Mrs Grandison-Clark was very proud of the fact that a number of the pupils had been chosen for leading roles in the West End.

Soon after the term started at The Royal Ballet School, I decided to go there one day and watch a boys' RAD syllabus class. Why I wanted to do that I will never know. I went to the studio where the boys were warming up, and sat down. About ten minutes passed, and still no teacher, so I said to the boys, 'let's not waste any more time, let us begin', and I took the class. The teacher did not arrive, so I thought he must have been held up by the traffic, and I just went home.

The next week, I went again and the same thing happened. This I knew was not normal and I decided to go and see Ursula Moreton, the principal, and told her what had happened. She said that she had just heard from the teacher of that class that he would no longer be able to take it, as he had been suddenly called to go away. I never asked who it was, but felt it must be an RAD examiner. But she said, 'I cannot give you the class to take, because you do not know the new syllabus.' Surprise, surprise! I was able to assure her that I did know the new syllabus, and that the two boys entering in Holland had just received Honours for both exams. 'Oh well,' she said, 'then you can take this class and one at White Lodge.' That was the beginning of my return to teaching at The Royal Ballet School.

My next move was to contact the Royal Academy of Dancing, with a view to becoming a Major Examiner. I had my first interview and was accepted to progress through the various stages.

One day when I was at The Royal Ballet School, I heard that one of the staff was expecting a baby and would be leaving at the end of the term, before Easter. I don't think this was in Madam's plan. Was this the opportunity I was waiting for? Was this why I had been led to go in to watch the boys' classes? I immediately went to see Ursula Moreton and told her that I had already been talking to Madam a few weeks before. I asked her if she would kindly remind Madam that I was here and would be very grateful if I could be considered for a teaching position in the school.

The message came through that they would like me to teach a Classical class in the Upper School, as part of my audition. This was quite a nerve-racking experience, being watched by Ailne Phillips,

Ursula Moreton and Barbara Fewster, who was now the Senior Ballet Mistress. Happily it all went well and I was given a letter inviting me to join the staff as a teacher of dancing, as from the commencement of the summer term 1962. This appointment would be regarded as probationary for that term.

I had been asking Mrs Grandison-Clark from the outset, if she would please give me a contract. Every time I saw her, she just said it would be coming. Now I had to tell her that I would not be able to teach for her after the end of the term. She was not at all pleased. What a blessing that she had not given me a contract. I then had to inform the RAD about not continuing with the Examiners Course.

After Easter, it was just wonderful to be back with the staff at The Royal Ballet School. I felt I was back where I belonged and would be able to pass on all that valuable knowledge that Madam had given me. Although I was still the youngest member of staff and regarded as such, in spite of the experience I had had in Holland, I was just so grateful not to be on my own any more. It was lovely to be able to discuss things with others and work together as a team.

My timetable consisted of a variety of classes. I was given the Senior I class which I was responsible for daily, and then the rest of my time was taken up teaching classes; like Solo Dances, Repertory Dances, Mime, Character, Virtuosity, and a number of Make-up classes, plus the RAD boys' Elementary, Intermediate and Advanced.

It was a very happy term for me, hard work, but in an atmosphere that I really enjoyed. That term went very quickly, because we had the annual test classes to arrange and of course there was the annual performance at the Royal Opera House. In those days all the staff had to go on stage at the end. It is now interesting to look at the photographs and see who was there at the time. The Summer Course that Madam used to give at the end of the term had finished several years before.

I was grateful to receive a letter in July to say they were very pleased with my work and asking me to remain with them for a further year. I did not actually receive a contract until about twenty years later!

In the autumn term, I now had two Classical classes to teach each day. They were the students who had just joined the school. I enjoyed helping them settle in and learn what a professional school was all about. Also, I had all the extra classes as before, except for

Character, which I was pleased about. It was now my duty to take all the auditions on a Tuesday evening, while the other members of staff took it by rota to do the judging.

Miss Edwards had now retired, but still kept teaching the RAD Advanced and Solo Seal exam classes and gave coaching to students who had been injured. The plan seemed to be that I would take over her RAD classes but prior to this she would go over the entire syllabus with me. This meant that she wanted me to dance through every exercise in the six years Course of Study, plus all the examination set exercises.

These lessons always took place at the end of my teaching day. Quite a challenge, but what a privilege to be working with such a wonderful teacher and to have her sharing with me all her valuable experience. It was a slightly strange feeling after having had her as a teacher when I was a student. The months went by and eventually we completed the task. With regard to the Solo Seal, I learnt it by attending all the classes, and it was wonderful to see the way Miss Edwards approached the solos.

I actually took over these classes in September 1963. Initially it was hard to stick to what one knew was correct, especially for the Advanced syllabus, when the students in front of me, who had come from all parts of the world, were doing it slightly differently. I had to be very clear in my own mind and just stick to it and say this is the way we are doing it here. Before long, Miss Edwards came in to watch one of my Advanced classes and afterwards she said 'well at least you can teach a *renversé*.' That was all! Thinking about it afterwards, I decided that movement was about one of the hardest things to teach and she must have meant it as a compliment.

Earlier during the spring term of 1963, Madam invited me to lunch. I must say my first thoughts were 'what have I done wrong?' but I soon came to my senses and realised it must be for some good reason. After I arrived at her home, she sat me down and said 'I am thinking of starting a Teachers' Course. Would you like to be at my side? Are you interested?' What an honour and privilege. Naturally, my answer was 'Yes please.'

I then told her more about the Teachers' Course I had been running in Holland, and about all the technical notes I had written about each exercise. She said they could be the basis for the technical theory classes she was expecting me to give as part of the programme. She also said she would like me to sit in on all the classes she would be teaching, and if she was unable to be there for some reason, she wanted me to take the classes.

Madam said she had decided to start the course by inviting students from my two Classical classes, who might be interested in teaching later, to attend the classes she would be giving. They would be divided into two groups, each group would have a special one hour class devoted to the ideas of teaching.

These classes were started in the autumn term 1963. There were fifteen students in Group 'A' Seniors and sixteen in Group 'B' Juniors. Again, wonderful for me to have this tremendous advantage of receiving all this first-hand knowledge from Madam.

In September 1963 Madam retired from being the Director of the Company and was now free to devote more of her time to the school, which included this idea of a Teachers' Course.

On the 7th of May 1964, there was a Gala Performance at the Royal Opera House in honour of Madam. After the performance, which included both companies, the lifts on the stage were raised to make a flight of stairs. Then the whole school and both companies, plus all the ballet staff, had to walk down these stairs in formation, before taking up their positions on either side of the stage. The staff were asked to wear black. It was a very moving moment when Madam appeared at the top of the stairs in a beautiful long turquoise evening dress. Then she slowly made her way down the stairs, acknowledging every one as she passed. When she reached the bottom, she was presented with a number of bouquets. I was so grateful to be part of this very special occasion.

Chapter 11

Early days of the Craftsman's Course

Prior to the official advertisement, Madam asked Ursula Moreton and me to devise a curriculum for a two-year course. A team of teachers (known to be the best in their field), were to be invited to contribute their expertise to the many discussions, and this included Mr John Allen, the Inspector appointed by the Department of Education and Science to The Royal Ballet School. These discussions took place before we started arranging the timetable.

During this time, Madam and I spent a number of hours going through the first three years of the RAD Course of Study. She felt they were very good for teaching children. However, she wanted to break down the exercises and give a clearer guide for their use. I wrote down all her suggestions and had them printed out for the students. These were to be incorporated into my Technical Theory classes.

Before starting these classes each year, I always gave the students a quotation from one of Tamara Karsavina's articles and this proved to be very helpful to them.

> Right thinking always helps the correctness of movement. If we understand the nature of the movement, our limbs follow our intellect and if we cultivate this relation between mind and body it will soon result in a correct instinct of movement.

In July 1964, The Royal Ballet School announced in the *Dancing Times* a Craftsman's Course for the Teaching of Ballet. This was a two-year course, with a third year by selection, devised by and under the supervision of Dame Ninette de Valois, designed to equip male and female students with a vocation for teaching with some of the important principles for the teaching of ballet.

The course started in September 1964, and the two classes were known as Craftsman's 'A' and Craftsman's 'B.'

The subjects and teachers involved with the timetable were:

Classical Ballet: Madam, Pamela May, Julia Farron, Barbara Fewster, Valerie Adams.

Classical Ballet Technical Theory, and Make-up: Valerie Adams.
RAD Major Ballet Syllabus, Advanced: Barbara Fewster, Valerie
    Adams.
RAD Intermediate and Elementary: Audrey Harman.
ISTD Cecchetti Ballet Syllabus: Nora Roche.
ISTD National, and History of Ballet : Joan Lawson.
Solo Dances, Repertory Dances, and Mime: Joy Newton.
Character: Maria Fay.
English Country Dancing and Scottish: June Wilson.
Music for Classical classes: Ena Child; and for Character classes:
    Mavis Barr.
Benesh Notation: Joan Benesh.

During 1964 and 1965 much of the pioneer work so far as the
practical teaching side was concerned, was done by Jean Alexander
and Elaine Welch, both from the original Group 'A.' They did a
tremendous amount to help the course get under way. They assisted
and taught the Preparatory and Form 1 classes at White Lodge, also
helping and teaching auditions. Both from Rhodesia, they left the
school in 1965 to return home to teach.

In the autumn term of 1965, more subjects were added to the
timetable:

Child Development Seminars: Mrs Branch and Miss Ruegg.
History of Drama: Graham Bowles.
Anatomy in Relation to the Dancer: Miss Staples to the 2nd and 3rd
    Years.
Classical Spanish to the 2nd and 3rd Years plus Theory for half an
    hour: Ana Ricarda.
Character Extra Class: Donald Britten.
RAD Childrens Grade Syllabus: Valerie Sunderland, 3rd Years go to
    RAD to join their students.
Highland Dancing Saturday morning : Miss Slade.
Teaching Practice for 3rd Years all at White Lodge teaching Form 1
    and 2.
Auditions 3rd Years teaching and 2nd Years watching and greeting
    parents.

A formal system of Examinations for the Diploma was being
evolved during this period, to be put into operation for 1966, when
the first diplomas were to be presented.

Reports were something else that had to be done at this time of the year. Madam said that I should write the 1st and 2nd Years and she would write the ones for those graduating, with me at her side. That was so interesting and I learnt a lot about writing reports. She wrote hers rather like a reference, looking into the future and stating the students' potential.

One student from the original 'A' Group and six from the 'B' Group, successfully completed the full programme. It was decided that because these students had been in the school for the year prior to the Craftsman's Course starting and had attended my Classical classes and those special lessons given by Madam on teaching, they should be the first recipients for the Three Year Diploma.

Prior to the first Diploma Presentations, Madam said to me that she did not want any fuss made of this occasion, but said 'I suppose we had better give them a drink and some crisps.'

On the day of the diploma presentations, Madam, Michael Wood, who was now Director of The Royal Ballet School; Ursula Moreton, Ballet Principal; Barbara Fewster, Senior Ballet Mistress; Graham Bowles, Head of Education; and myself, were gathered in the office which Madam used, to receive the seven graduates. A very exciting day in the history of the course.

Mr Wood read out the names and Madam presented the diplomas, giving her congratulations to all. Everyone was then offered a drink. Madam said her gift to the graduates was to allow them to watch classes, either at the Upper or Lower Schools. She always said how important it was to keep one's 'eye in,' in other words, to keep up to date with what was going on. All they had to do, was to telephone and check that it would be convenient. This still continues to this very day.

Afterwards I decided that a photograph should be taken so that I would remember what they looked like and so I took one with my Brownie Box camera.

Four of the graduates had decided to have some stage experience first before going into teaching and the other three took teaching positions straight away.

In the autumn term of 1966 I dropped one of my Classical classes on the Dancer's Course in order to devote more time to the Craftsman's Course, as it was my responsibility to see that this rather complicated timetable ran smoothly.

This term changes and additions were made to the timetable: Madam wanted the RAD classes to be taught by examiners, and Jean Bedells and Iris Truscott were engaged to teach these classes. I was pleased because it took the responsibility away from me. I still had the Solo Seal classes on the Dancers Course, which I was pleased about, as Miss Edwards had guided me through every facet of what was required, and I really enjoyed working with the students on these dances.

In the spring term William Bundy from the Royal Opera House was asked to arrange lectures for the 2nd and 3rd Years on Stage Craft and Lighting.

Mr Ivor Robertson, the Orthopaedic Surgeon for the company, took over the anatomy lectures, giving six to the 1st Years and six to the 2nd Years.

Lawrence Bradbury from the Tate Gallery was asked to give art lectures and he also arranged a tour of the Tate Gallery for the students each year. These lectures were so popular with the students and continued until I retired.

Madam continued teaching her Wednesday morning class.

In October a staff meeting was held with all the teachers involved with the course and each discussed their classes' advantages and disadvantages. Then I had to make any necessary changes to the timetable.

Ursula Moreton was very keen that our graduates should receive full recognition, like teachers in educational schools. So negotiations began to link the Craftsman's Course with that of a College of Education. The case was presented in the summer of 1967 to a standing committee at the Institute of Education at the University of London.

In the first instance the link was to be with Gipsy Hill College in Kingston and discussions were held at meetings which Michael Wood, Ursula Moreton, Graham Bowles and myself attended.

Diploma Day 1967 had arrived and the procedure was the same as the previous year. This time there were just three graduates. One of them wanted to dance first before taking a teaching position. The other two, one from the USA and one from Hong Kong, returned to their own countries and both went straight into teaching.

* * *

In September 1967 I became General Assistant to the Craftsman's Course and gave up all my classes on the Dancer's Course, except for the RAD Solo Seal.

There were again timetable changes; I now had responsibility for teaching the first Classical class each morning. On Mondays, I had the 2nd and 3rd Years together and taught Madam's Advanced Syllabus. The other days, I had all three years together. Because it was such a large class of thirty plus, I was allowed to use the Covent Garden studio before the company came in at 10.15 a.m. a wonderful space in which to be able to move. This studio, the size of Covent Garden stage, had been built together with several other studios while I was away in Holland, and the company was now in residence with all their offices at Barons Court. This all created a wonderful atmosphere for the students, to be passing Margot Fonteyn and Rudolf Nureyev and all the other company members in the corridors and in the canteen. There was also a small window in the door of the studio where one could watch the company working.

Each day, a couple of the 3rd Years would go and join one of the Dancers' Course classes. I was now also teaching the 1st and 2nd Year Solo Dances, plus 1st Year Mime. Julia Farron would take 2nd Year Mime. Valerie Sunderland and Walter Trevor taught the Character to replace Maria Fay, and Speech Training was now also included.

In November, a meeting was held at Kings College, London, with a proposed course of training for students of the Craftsman's Course, in conjunction with Gipsy Hill College of Education. Our application for official recognition was dealt with by a standing sub-committee representing Physical Education, which ultimately gave its approval to the course at The Royal Ballet School, accepting Ballet as equivalent to a main subject in the courses of the College of Education.

This was the year that 'The Massine Course on the Theory of Composition' was introduced. Léonide Massine came to structure and lay down the contents of his course and Audrey Harman was assisting him. The first year commenced in May 1968 and six of the 1st Year students were involved. There were three one and a quarter hours sessions, Monday to Friday for two weeks. This, of course disrupted the timetable in more ways than one.

Diploma Day 1968 had arrived and the procedure was as before. This year there were five graduates. One of them decided to dance first and the rest went straight into teaching.

At the end of the summer term Ursula Moreton retired as Ballet Principal and her place was taken by Barbara Fewster. I had always admired Barbara as an excellent teacher. We first met when she came to the Wessex School of Dancing to give the students a class. She had originally come from the same school when it was run by Miss Hooley and our paths had crossed a number of times. Now we would be working closely together Madam always remarked that it was amazing that we had come from the same school.

Looking at the autumn term timetable, it was now very full and I had to keep a close eye on how it was working. The Massine Course, taught by Audrey Harman was scheduled into the timetable; two and three quarter hours per week for the 1st and 2nd Years. Mr Massine returned in November to continue with his course.

3rd Year students embarked on their first outside teaching practice. Requests for help came from examiners, who needed replacements for their classes while they were away examining. This brought students from the course in contact with children outside the school for the first time.

For the regional auditions in Bristol, Coventry, Liverpool, Glasgow, one of the 3rd Year students would accompany Ursula Moreton and take the auditions. The same thing happened when I went to Newcastle and York.

During November at the request of one of the chief Inspectors of Physical Education, Michael Wood, Ursula Moreton and I visited schools in the ILEA area, to watch their classes on 'dance'. When I watched these classes I began to wonder how our students could possibly fit into such a situation, when the demands of the Craftsman's Course were for a much higher standard.

In the new year René Bon came to the school as a guest teacher for about six weeks. He gave master classes and I watched as much as I could. He had many different ideas about teaching ballet. His classes were two hours in length and the barre work very slow. It was never shorter than one hour. Sometimes I wondered if the dancers were ever going to jump. However, in spite of all this I know I did learn a lot from him.

For Diploma Day 1969, Madam suggested that the former graduates should be invited to watch the graduates class on the Dancer's Course, taken by Eileen Ward. She felt this was a way of them keeping their 'eye in,' and up to date with the standard required. This would take place prior to the diploma presentations.

The presentation ceremony was held in the Baylis Hall, since a number of former graduates were attending to support those graduating. We also needed more space for the reception which was also to be on a grander scale than previously.

I had been able to purchase two long white tablecloths which could be wiped over and used again, to cover the three trestle tables which would be placed down one side of the studio. We also had attractive paper plates, napkins and flowers. The school provided funds for the 1st and 2nd Years to be able to make sandwiches, savouries, cakes etc. and provide drinks. A number of them went out the day before to pick strawberries from the fields and this became quite a tradition. They were at the school very early to make the sandwiches and be sure that everything was organised and ready on time. When all was laid out it looked so inviting and I think the 1st and 2nd Years felt proud to be responsible for such an event, and to know that one day, others would be doing it for them.

There were eleven graduates that year. All were going into teaching and the one from Thailand would be dancing as well. Deborah Sims, one of those graduating, was engaged to help me in the office for two years and to take a few classes. In the autumn term, there were very few changes to be made to the timetable, which showed that things were beginning to settle down. Doris Bishop, the wardrobe mistress, gave lessons to the 2nd Years, on how to make a tutu and ballet skirt, something very useful for them to know, and they wore them for their Solo Dances examination.

The school arranged for me to have a series of private coaching sessions from Eileen Ward, which was a great privilege as I admired her very much. I was always keen to learn as much as I could from other teachers, in order to be able to pass on this knowledge to my students.

Diploma Day 1970 was all arranged as the previous year, as that had been so successful. Naturally, there would now be more graduates attending each year. Again, the 1st and 2nd Years did all the preparations for the reception and made it a memorable occasion for those graduating.

There were seven graduates and all went into teaching. I still had the help of Deborah Sims, which I was grateful for, as I was teaching three or four classes a day, plus all the other things I was responsible for, so I was certainly glad to have some help.

This was the year that the *Newsletter* was started, giving all the names and addresses of the graduates from the beginning of the course. Each year they would be asked to send in their up-to-date news and what they were doing. In those days it was quite a complicated job, because it had to be typed out on to a stencil, then painted with black ink before going onto a roller. After that, the number of copies were then rolled out by turning the handle of the machine. So different from the easy way of today!

The timetable changes which took place in the autumn term included the introduction of the GCE 'O' level Ballet classes for the 1st and 2nd Year students, in preparation for them to take the examination in May 1972. This examination would in future be a compulsory requirement for the diploma. I now had the assistance of former graduate Deirdre Watts to help me in the office and take a few classes.

Richard Gregson took over from William Bundy to arrange the Royal Opera House lectures. These were always very much appreciated and he continued arranging them until the course closed in 2000.

The 3rd Years were also very privileged to be allowed to watch ballet performances from the wings at the Royal Opera House. Each season, two students were allowed a pass at each performance. They had to stick strictly to all the backstage rules, or this privilege would be withdrawn.

The 3rd Years continued to teach at all the auditions, including the Lower School Finals, with 2nd Years assisting and watching.

Diploma Day 1971. The number of graduates coming to watch Eileen Ward's graduates' class on the Dancers' Course was now mounting.

The presentation ceremony carried on as before, as did the reception. There were just three graduates that year. Two were going to dance with the company in Rheims and Jane Slocombe was offered a teaching position at the Elmhurst Ballet School, the first time one of our graduates had been accepted into a professional school. That year we had a photographer to take pictures of Madam with the three graduates.

The ground work had now been laid for the course and we were all looking forward to the next chapter in its history.

Chapter 12

Director of The Teachers' Training Course

In the autumn term of 1971 Madam made me the Course Director. The course in future would be known as The Royal Ballet School Teachers' Training Course. Graduates were informed to change the letters after their name to Dip. RBS (TTC).

As we were very short on space, alterations were made in the Baylis Hall. Where there had previously been a balcony from which classes could be watched, that was closed and several study rooms were made for lessons. Where there had been a platform with a piano, that was closed to make an office for me. This was a great improvement because prior to these changes I had shared an office with a secretary and having private interviews with students there was not easy to arrange. In my office it was lovely and bright, having windows on two sides. With some attractive curtains, it was a happy place to be, in spite of hearing the music coming from the studio.

The three-year course had now emerged in what was to be its permanent form, following the years of work given to it by Madam and Ursula Moreton, whose aim to gain proper remuneration for the teacher of ballet and enable students to gain full teacher status within the state system, had been realised.

There were again timetable changes. The Child Development Seminars were taken over by James Burch and Leslie Righley of the Institute of Education and the work was carried out within the terms of the possible linked course with Battersea College.

The Music Course was extended and taken over by Dame Ruth Railton, the founder of the National Youth Orchestra. The Anatomy Lectures were taken over by Kenneth Backhouse, former head of the Royal College of Surgeons. He was very interested in ballet and gave his lectures in such a way as to be of real help to the teacher of ballet. He stayed until I retired in 1995.

The RAD Grade Syllabus was taken over by Madeleine Sharp, who from time to time brought in the children from her own school to give demonstrations of the work. Jean Bedells took over all the

Major Syllabus. Benesh Notation was now to be taught by Lorna Mossford and Susan Smith, a graduate from the Craftsman's Course in 1969, who was very interested in this work and had done further studies to gain her teaching qualifications. Supported Adage was added for the 3rd Years and taught by Keith Lester. Contempory Dance classes were added too, for the 2nd and 3rd Years, but English and Scottish dancing had to be dropped, mainly due to the pressure of work.

Cecchetti Advanced for the Student Teacher was now introduced by Nora Roche for the 3rd Years, and two graduates in 1972 left the course with this examination and the RAD Advanced. This was now to be aimed at as a future goal, because that meant they were fully qualified to teach either syllabus in any school.

The Teaching Practice classes which I taught, proved to be a very successful way of introducing the students to actual teaching, often a very scary thought of standing in front of a class. All the 2nd Years would work with the 1st Years on a one-to-one basis, and I would walk round the studio listening to their comments and guiding when necessary. We started with all the basic barre exercises and then moved into the centre, where a 2nd Year would take three or more of the 1st Years, having to expand their vision and see more than one person moving. The others would be watching and developing their eye to see faults at the same time. This we proved was an excellent way of starting the teaching and for the students to gain confidence when imparting their knowledge.

On the 12th of February my father came home as he was now retired from the sea. This was a time of adjustment after all those years of his being away. However, he was able to get a job with a shipping company as a Port Captain in Portsmouth docks, which enabled him to go on board ships even though he did not go to sea. We were able to have a car, which we all drove, and during the next eleven years we shared many happy times together.

The Massine Course now had examinations in place. The Royal Ballet School was the examining board for Great Britain and Northern Ireland and issued the one and only Diploma. The examinations would be held at The Royal Ballet School for the 3rd Year TTC.

The Craftsman's Award, donated by Dr and Mrs Hoare, was in gratitude for the training their daughter Judith had received while on the course. They wished the name Craftsman's to be kept. Dr and Mrs Hoare very kindly continued giving this award for the next twenty-three years until I retired.

Diploma Day 1972 was arranged in a slightly different way from the previous year. Former graduates watched the Dancers Course' graduates class taken by Eileen Ward. Then parents, who were invited for the first time, former graduates and staff gathered in the Baylis Hall. They were then treated to a Spanish dance by Tina Young and Deborah Phillips. Ana Ricarda felt that they had achieved such a high standard of the Spanish work that it should be seen by an audience.

The reception then went ahead while those two changed. This occasion was now turning into something special and the graduates were appearing in dresses and outfits bought especially for the day. The presentation of diplomas then followed as in previous years. Dr and Mrs Hoare gave their award and Madam gave her usual congratulations. For the first time, the head student gave her thanks on behalf of the rest of those graduating, and that was to be the beginning of another tradition which was to continue throughout the years.

There were twelve graduates that year, the largest number so far. Four of them wanted to dance first and the rest decided to go straight into teaching. Tina Young was accepted to teach at the Bush Davies, another professional school. The photograph taken of the group with Madam and myself was still in black and white.

In the autumn term, it was good to feel that the timetable was now well organised and that only slight adjustments would be necessary. Unfortunately I did not have anyone to help me that year.

In the *Newsletter*, Michael Wood sent this notice to the graduates:

The Royal Ballet School Teachers' Training Course has now been officially accepted by the University of London as comparable to a main course at a College of Education. Those students who have gained the Diploma and who also have the necessary academic qualifications may now go to Battersea College of Education for a one year shortened course, upon the successful completion of which, they would have qualified Teacher Status.

One day in February 1973 I received a telephone call from Mr van Vlijman, the new Director of the Koninklijk Conservatorium. I must say I was totally amazed when he said, 'we want you to give up your job in London and return to Holland, because the Government is about to close the Ballet School. No students have joined the company since you left twelve years ago, and that is the purpose of the school.' He then said that he was coming to London the following weekend to discuss it with me. I had no intention of giving up my job and told him not to come. He was still very persistent, but I could understand that he had a big problem. Another week passed and he called again, this time offering me double my salary. That was quite something, but I did not want to leave The Royal Ballet School where I felt I really belonged.

I then began to wonder what on earth had happened to that Ballet School, which had been running so smoothly, with students joining the company each year. I knew a little bit of my heart was still there and it made me consider if there was any way that I could help. Around April each year, Léonide Massine gave my Teacher's Course students the special Course on Composition and this always disrupted the timetable. It came to me that perhaps this was the time that I could go over to Holland and see what was going on. I received permission from Michael Wood and telephoned Mr van Vlijman with my suggestion that I would go over for two weeks. He was delighted with the idea and he himself visited The Royal Ballet School to talk to me, watch classes, and meet Michael Wood.

My mother accompanied me, and we flew to Holland on the 29th of April. I now found that a new studio had been built in the old school at the Lombardstraat, which was a great improvement and that a large stage had been built in one of the 'hidden churches' just near the Koninklijk Conservatorium. This made an excellent place for giving class and could be used for performances, as it had plenty of raised seating.

After the first two days of watching the classes, I still did not know what the problem was. It was only when I taught them on the third day that I began to realise what was wrong. They found it very difficult to pick up even the simple exercises I was giving them, so it was no wonder that they were not able to go through the company auditions. On my way back to the tram I was wondering how this could be. It suddenly came to me that it was like having a little dog on a lead for eight years and then letting it off to run. Of course it would not know how. There has to be self discipline, but what I had seen was so rigid and restricted that they were not moving freely.

It was certainly hard teaching them but gradually I could see an improvement and felt we were on the right lines.

On the following Tuesday I was called to a meeting in the Director's office. I had not been told what it was all about and when I arrived I was surprised to see all the heads of the Koninklijk Conservatorium sitting round the oval table. After I had taken my seat, Mr van Vlijman stood up and said 'Miss Adams will you please open the meeting and give us your opinion of the Ballet School.' That was a shock, I certainly was not prepared after only a week and had not yet made any official notes. I paused for a few moments and after standing up found myself giving them a long list of things which I felt were necessary to have in place before progress could be made. When I had finished, Mr van Vlijman thanked me very much and said that everything I had suggested had been noted and would be implemented by next year, if I would return then to see the progress. I remember rushing back to the hotel, hoping that I could remember what I had said, because I then had to write to the Minister of Arts and give my report. This was an experience never to be forgotten.

The improvement continued during the rest of the second week and there was an opportunity to talk to the teachers. My former student and assistant, Hanneke, had retired from dancing with the company and was now teaching with them. One of my suggestions was that whoever was running the school should have their home and family in Holland so that there could be some stability, rather than having someone from another country, who would probably only want to stay a couple of years.

After returning to London I started to receive telephone calls from the Head of Dance asking for advice, but I had to say that in no way could I run the school from the other side of the water. He did visit London during the year and was able to watch classes, which was good, because it helped him to understand what I was talking about.

Diploma Day 1973 and the presentations followed the same pattern as the previous year. However, in place of the Spanish dance, the graduates showed a Georgian dance arranged by Valerie Sunderland. There were six graduates that year, two wanting to dance first and the other four deciding to take a teaching position.

In the autumn term, for the first time, there were no changes to the timetable.

In January 1974 a letter was sent to the graduates inviting them to apply for the one-year course at Battersea College of Education to start in September 1974.

In May I returned to Holland for twelve days, to see how the Ballet School was progressing since my visit the previous year, and to give further advice. The wonderful news was that three of the students had joined the company, which was very encouraging for all, especially for me to be able to put it in my report to the Minister of Arts, as well as the positive progress that had been made.

Later in the year Ellen Brusse, one of the teachers, came to watch classes at The Royal Ballet School, both at White Lodge and Barons Court, and this proved to be most helpful to her.

The examination procedure for The Royal Ballet School Teachers' Training Course Diploma, now consisted of examinations held internally and examined by experts in their particular field. Of the ten examinations set, six had to be passed in order to qualify for the diploma. This was in addition to the required standards being obtained in the RAD, Cecchetti and National examinations.

Diploma Day 1974. Former graduates were invited again to watch a class on the Dancers Course, this time taught by Nancy Kilgour, prior to the presentations.

Everyone then gathered in the Baylis Hall, but there was no sign of Madam. I telephoned her and she had made a mistake about the date in her diary. She told me to go down to the company offices and find a member of the company to present the diplomas, and that she would be along as soon as possible. Monica Mason kindly agreed to do the honours. Madam did arrive most apologetically and congratulated all the graduates. I made sure in the future that I actually checked the date in her diary to see that it was correct. That year there were seven graduates. Two wanted to have stage experience before teaching and the other five went straight into teaching.

The course had now been running for ten years and had established a very strong group of graduates, with the highest standard of work to date.

Timetable changes for the autumn term included the music lessons for the 1st and 2nd Years being taken over by Veronica Clayton, and Thomas McLelland Young, the pianist who always played for my Friday morning class, would take the 3rd Years. He could then help them in various ways from his point of view as a class pianist. He was also an organist and would take the students along to the local church, and play, explaining to them how the organ worked. Also a composer, he had won many awards both here and abroad. We were to work together for twenty-nine years. He always seemed to know exactly the type of music that I needed. Our Friday morning class became very popular, with former graduates coming to watch.

The Benesh Notation classes were now taught by Hilary Condron, who stayed until the course closed. The Benesh Notation Teaching Diploma was introduced and gained by three of the 3rd Years that year. Susan Smith, the graduate who had been teaching for us, went to South Africa to the CAPAB to be the Company Choreologist.

In addition, there were three former graduates to take the one year Special Course at Battersea College of Education.

In April I visited the Ballet School in Holland and it was once again good to see the positive progress that had been made. This time I was able to give a more comprehensive and detailed report to the teachers, who, I felt, could now understand what I was trying to encourage them to do. As before, I sent my report to the Minister of Arts.

That year I decided to present an award to the Bournemouth Musical Festival, considering that it was that competition at the end of May 1944 that really set my career on the path which was to follow. It is called The Valerie Adams Award and is a silver plate, which is presented to the candidate showing the most potential for classical ballet. The names of the winners are inscribed on it and they are able to keep it for just one year. The award now also includes a cheque and whenever possible I try to be there to present it. Over the years there have been some really talented dancers who have done well with their careers.

On Diploma Day 1975 the presentations and reception were held in the Garden Room Studio because the Baylis Hall was no longer large enough for all the people who were attending the occasion. Amongst the graduates there were two from America and they desired to have more sweet things served at the reception and made a number themselves. That year we also celebrated the first three graduates to complete the course at Battersea College successfully.

Out of the eight graduates that year, one decided to have stage experience first and six went straight into teaching, one of them joining Tina Young at the Bush Davies school. One decided to take the course at Battersea College and the two from America returned to their own country.

In the autumn term 1975 we missed having Eileen Ward on the ballet staff as she had left to move elsewhere. She had contributed greatly to the school and I for one was very sad to see her go.

One Sunday during this term I was invited by the Bournemouth Ballet Club, where I had been an original member in 1947, to give two classes, a junior and senior class at the Municipal College Hall. I had been on a previous occasion in 1968 when Madam asked me to deputise for her. I must say it was quite a strange feeling to be teaching these classes in the hall where I had attended classes all those years ago and it brought back many happy memories. This I continued to do for the next several years.

In February 1976 Noreen Bush invited me to visit the Bush Davies School in East Grinstead. It was a most enjoyable day watching classes and talking with her. I was able to tell her that it was because of her placing me first in the Ballet Class at the Musical Festival, that I was able to receive my first watch when I was twelve and she certainly laughed at that. While there I also saw the students she was shortly going to send up for auditions at The Royal Ballet School. I was so pleased that she had already accepted several of our graduates to teach for her as I knew what a high standard she required.

Towards the end of the following April I returned to Holland. It was good to see that noticeable progress had been made since my last visit and to hear the wonderful news that again three more students had been accepted into the company. It proved that the school was now running successfully and my reports to the Minister of Arts were favourable.

At the end of June Hanneke and Ellen came over from the Ballet School in Holland to watch classes at White Lodge as the students were the same age as the ones they were teaching. Also, one of the pianists came to sit in on classes and hear the type of music being played.

That year, the two former graduates who had attended Battersea College successfully completed that course.

Diploma Day 1976 followed the plan of the previous year. Nancy Kilgour took the class for the former graduates to watch and then the presentations and the reception were held in the Garden Room Studio.

The eight graduates had achieved a new record because they were leaving us with the RAD Advanced Certificate and the Cecchetti Advanced Student Teaching Certificate. All went straight into teaching except for the one who was going to Battersea College. The Bush Davies school asked to have another graduate from us and also one was accepted by the Hammond school, the professional school in Chester. For me the best thing was to have one of the graduates, Hope Keelen, as my assistant.

In the autumn term there seemed to be more timetable changes to deal with, but how grateful I was to have Hope to help me. In her, I had found a good organiser – someone who could easily fall into the way I had everything planned. Otherwise it would have been hopeless because everything had to run to a very strict format, or it just could not work. The thirty-eight examinations during the year that had to be arranged and examiners found, was only one of our many challenges.

Jocelyn Mather was now teaching the 1st and 2nd Years for Cecchetti, leaving Nora Roche to just take the 3rd Years. Hope Keelan was teaching the RAD Elementary and Intermediate, 1st Year Grade Work and Speech.

The Massine Course was now dropped and Richard Glasstone gave lectures to the 3rd Years on Choreography. As part of the course, Madam wanted them to choreograph a classical and *demi-caractère* solo, which she would then make comments on to the students. She said it was very important that they should be able to arrange these dances in case they were required at some stage to enter candidates for the Musical Festival. I think the students sometimes found her comments hard to digest.

In January I was invited by the Royal Academy of Dancing to give two lectures on Grooming for Class during their Special Week. It seemed that some teachers were having difficulty in encouraging their pupils to turn up looking neat for class. Their questions afterwards were unbelievable because to me it was always the teacher's responsibility to instil the necessary discipline.

At the end of April I made my trip to Holland staying eleven days and it was good to see that progress was being maintained. The usual report was again written.

In June Hanneke and Ellen made another visit to The Royal Ballet School for a week. Watching the classes there was proving to be most beneficial.

On the 29th and 30th of June the first Accreditation and Inspection of the Teachers' Training Course by the Department of Education and Science took place. Happily everything went very well and we received a good report.

Earlier in the year those graduating appeared at my office door in a group. I said to them 'what is this, mutiny?' But no, they wanted to ask if it would be possible to show a class in front of their parents. They said their parents had given up so much for them to be there and it was only fair that they should see a little of what they had to go through. I asked Madam, and she agreed that I should give the class for their parents to watch in the Garden Room Studio. All the former graduates would be watching a class in another studio as usual.

Diploma Day 1977. On that day of all days, I was held up in traffic and was late for the class, however, the graduates all carried on regardless as they had been trained to do, and they were happy to have shown their parents the class that we had prepared for the occasion. They were then given half an hour to change, while Hope and I prepared the Garden Room Studio for the presentations.

There were eight graduates that year. One of them wanted to continue her studies in preparation to become a physiotherapist and one joined a ballet company in West Germany. The Bush Davies school offered another position to one of the graduates. One was going to join her sister who ran a dancing school and two were emigrating, one to New Zealand and the other to Canada, where they had been offered teaching positions. The Stella Mann School offered a position, as did the Academy of Ballet in Edinburgh.

The reception was held in the Baylis Hall, so while I was teaching, Hope was able to get everything organised for that.

Three former graduates who had successfully completed the course at Battersea College were also present. Unfortunately, this was the last time that our graduates would be able to do the course, because the government closed it down.

On Tuesday the 26th of July together with Julia Farron and Alfred Rodrigues, her husband, and Marion Lane, I was invited to an Afternoon Party in the garden of Buckingham Palace. What a thrilling experience that was, and especially as it was the year of the Silver Jubilee. It was quite a cool afternoon but lovely to be able to walk all around the gardens and enjoy this very special occasion.

At the end of the term, on the Friday, Michael Wood was retiring. He had been a good director and had supported me well, and I was sorry to see him leave. James Monahan would become director in the autumn term.

That same day after lunch, my mother and father and I drove down to Taunton for Hope's wedding to Philip on the Saturday. Some time before this she had asked my mother if we could be her family. As her parents had come over from Canada for her graduation the previous year, they could not make it over again. She asked if my father could give her away and of course he was delighted to do so. As soon as he agreed, he went off and had a new lightweight suit made.

The weather had not been good that summer and Hope kept telling me that she was determined to walk back from the church to the reception at Philip's home. In fact it turned out to be a lovely day and one certainly enjoyed by all. To me, seeing Hope with my father, was like seeing the younger sister I never had.

In the autumn term there were no changes, except for adding Dalcroze Eurhythmics. It was decided that we needed to incorporate this subject to help the students with their music knowledge, especially when teaching children, and Elizabeth Vanderspar was asked to give these lessons.

I was now Barbara Fewster's 'unofficial' deputy, and in spite of having Hope, the workload was really getting quite heavy because it meant going down to White Lodge more often and attending all the assessment classes at the Upper School, on top of my commitments with the course. The auditions were just an ongoing thing and my next trip was to Manchester in October.

The following April I was unable to visit Holland due to the extra work. However, two more students had been accepted for the main company and one for the Nederlands Dans Theater, so that was good news. Later in the year, Hanneke, Ellen and Wim visited The Royal Ballet School again.

Diploma Day 1978. As there were only three graduates that year, we just followed the pattern we had in place for the year before last. The presentations and reception were held in the Garden Room Studio. The two girls graduating wanted to have stage experience before teaching and the one boy, who had been a professional, wanted to teach in South Africa.

The timetable changes for this year included Nora Roche retiring from teaching. What an excellent teacher she had been and had contributed so much to the course. Tina Young, one of our graduates who had completed the course and gained her teaching qualifications at Battersea College, now took over the Child Development classes.

In February 1979 I went down to the Bush Davies School in East Grinstead to hold an audition there and took with me as my helper Caroline Jenkins, a 3rd Year student who had originally been one of their students. It was nice having someone with me who knew her way around.

That month the Accreditation and Inspection of the Teachers' Training Course by the Department of Education and Science took place once again and as before, everything went well.

In the middle of May I made another visit to Holland, but I could only spare the time for one week. It happened to be a difficult time for all concerned, because one of their pupils had gone missing just before I arrived. They had thought about cancelling my visit but decided to let it stand. It was certainly a time to keep very calm and positive and to do my best to lift up the atmosphere and help when and wherever I could. They told me afterwards that they were so pleased that I was there to give them all support. Again, I received the good news that three of the students had been accepted into the Nederlands Dans Theater.

Madam agreed that the Teachers' Course Library should be named after her. She contributed the money she had received from her Erasmus Award, which enabled us to purchase two cupboards. A number of books were also given by Madam, who wanted them kept under lock and key. Originally these cupboards were in the Study Room with a special photograph of Madam hanging there. However, when Graham Bowles retired, they were placed in my office and I then had the pleasure of looking at that lovely photograph.

The graduates leaving us that year decided to start 'The de Valois Cassette Library Fund,' to enable the students on the course to have a cassette recorder and tapes to help them when practising. The school could not afford to pay for this. The fund was ongoing for a number of years on Diploma Day and much gratitude was expressed for the many people who signed the book and contributed to the fund.

Diploma Day 1979 marked the giving of the 100th diploma,

a special occasion in the history of the course. There were to be fourteen graduates that year, the largest number and of the highest standard recorded so far.

To celebrate this special occasion, the diploma presentations were held late afternoon in the Covent Garden Studio. As well as Madam, special guests were invited, including Dame Alicia Markova, Winifred Edwards, Miss Curling, and my mother for the first time, plus parents, former graduates, and the staff.

I gave a classical class to the graduates, and this was followed by a Performance of Dances, with Tom Young at the piano. Mr Wilson, the caretaker, provided special lighting. The graduates were then given the usual half hour to prepare themselves for the presentations.

The reception was held in the Baylis Hall Studio, conveniently situated close by. Again the 1st and 2nd Years arranged a delicious spread, including freshly picked strawberries. This really was the largest affair to date and a promise of what was to follow in the future.

The fourteen graduates that year were all well placed. Five received contracts with ballet companies in Europe, and often found that when there, they had opportunities to teach as well. One wished to continue studies at The Place, and another at the Benesh Institute, while doing some part time teaching elsewhere. The other seven were offered teaching positions here and abroad. The one from Thailand, was going back to join the two graduates who were already teaching at the Fine Arts Department in Bangkok.

Barbara Fewster had sent me a telegram. 'Congratulations to you and the course on reaching your one hundredth diploma this day.' Afterwards, Miss Edwards sent me a card of congratulations and a charming little pottery basket of flowers. To receive that from her, has always meant so much to me!

We had passed another landmark in the history of the course and were ready for the exciting possibilities which now lay ahead.

Chapter 13

Progress of The Teachers' Training Course

Towards the end of the summer holidays each year, Barbara Fewster and I would sit down together and try to work out our various timetables and blend them into one. By now my timetable was more or less set with the twenty plus teachers, the majority being freelance so their times could not be changed. It gradually came to the point when my timetable had to be laid out first and Barbara was having to arrange the Dancers' Course around it. We spent many hours allocating all the classes to the seven studios available and of course there had to be give and take on both sides. Then there were the teachers and pianists to sort out. That was a challenge in itself. I always remember Barbara looking at me one day and saying 'you need food'! She seemed to be able to survive on a Kit Kat, where I needed something more substantial.

In the autumn term of 1979, our timetable had few changes, except for adding some classes in Dalcroze Eurythmics which were given by Mrs van der Spar. These classes really did help the students gain a deeper understanding of music, and what they were learning would be of such help when they were teaching children. I remembered that Madam had these classes in the timetable when I first started teaching, and that it had been a compulsory subject for all students, both music and dance, at the Koninklijk Conservatorium in Holland. The other change was that Valerie Sunderland had now returned to take over the character classes after having her two children.

The de Valois Cassette Library Fund started by the previous years' graduates had raised up to £400, so we were able to purchase a good selection of tapes of the various syllabuses that the students were studying, and these proved to be so helpful.

It was during this term that I decided I must get a 'Snoopy.' Every morning on my way to the school, I was held up in traffic outside a corner shop that had its window full of Snoopys, big ones, small ones, they had them all. For anyone who does not know, it was the beagle dog in the cartoon 'Peanuts' by Charles M Schulz. I thought if

I could have one just six inches tall, to have as a travelling companion in the car, that would be fine. Well, one day, with my mother I went along to the shop. What a choice! Somehow, though, they did not have the size I was looking for, but we came away with one twelve inches in height which had a lovely expression on its face. As we left the shop, the assistant said: 'don't you want any clothes?' Oh no, we didn't want any clothes! Well, to cut a long story short, we did go back and get a sailor suit and later the wardrobe of clothes became larger.

One Christmas, I decided to take Snoopy into the school on the last day of term, in a Father Christmas outfit, together with a bag of sweets. The students saw me in a different light that day, because I liked to make Snoopy move, so it looked as though he was responding to what everyone said. Of course, they liked that and from then on, I had to make sure he was always with me on that day. One year my students from Japan bought me one from a limited edition. Well, this really did start something I could never have dreamed of, because soon after, I started receiving Snoopys from all over the world and now have a collection of over two hundred and fifty of all shapes and sizes and a variety of memorabilia. What fun!

At the school in my office I had a Snoopy poster on the door, which showed a picture of Snoopy on a skateboard, and across the top was written 'Think Style'. At times, when perhaps an interview with a student had not been that easy, before they left the room, I would always say 'have you looked at Snoopy recently?' And of course, that would make them laugh and they would leave on a happy note.

After returning from the Easter break in 1980, I had to tell Barbara that I could no longer be her 'unofficial' deputy, as running the course and teaching was more than enough to deal with, in spite of having Hope giving me such strong support.

That year, I was also unable to visit the Ballet School in Holland and missed the opening of the new building at the Koninklijk Conservatorium. However, the good news was that students continued to join the companies.

Diploma Day 1980 followed the same procedure as the previous year, the only real change was having the class and performance in the Sadler's Wells Studio. My mother started another tradition which was to continue until 2000, by giving those graduating and the pianists involved, a carnation to wear. The graduates all seemed to look forward to the moment when they put them on.

That year Madam also added another special touch to things, by giving a signed copy of one of the books she had written to the graduate who had received The Highest Examination Results. This was given at the time of presenting the Awards. Also, we now had the services of a professional photographer, Michael Martin, the father of Lorna, who was graduating. He was for many years to give his services to the school and took a number of coloured photographs during the whole proceedings, so that the graduates had some lovely pictures to remind them of their special occasion.

There were eight graduates that year. One decided to go to Southampton Technical College, but would be doing some part-time teaching. Four others had teaching positions to go to and the other three had dancing contracts.

In the autumn term of 1980 the main change was that Joan Lawson, who had been teaching the National classes for us since the beginning of the course, was retiring. What dedicated and faithful service she had given us, making sure that all the students were well prepared for their National examinations. She had also given a number of other lectures on various topics to do with ballet training, which had been so helpful to the students. She was a special friend of mine. I had known her since she gave the first classes to the Bournemouth Ballet Club in 1947. Vivienne Saxton, a former graduate, took over all the National classes and proved to be a worthy successor.

Denise Winmill, who had been on the course at the very beginning but had decided to leave after two years because she was offered a dancing contract with the Sadler's Wells Opera Ballet, telephoned me one day during the previous term. After talking for a time and her telling me about her dancing school, I suggested that she might consider returning to complete the last year of the course. This is what she decided to do and it was good to have her on the course again.

During this year, a One Year Teaching Course for Professional Dancers was advertised. It was to be run at The Royal Ballet School and was fully approved by the Directors of The Royal Ballet and the Sadler's Wells Royal Ballet.

1981 was another year when I did not visit the Ballet School in Holland. However, there were good reports that students were entering the companies.

Diploma Day went ahead as before, but this year we had the advantage of having the Covent Garden Studio because the company was away. After I gave the usual classical class with the graduates in front of their parents, Madam, Dame Alicia Markova, and other invited guests watched the graduates showing a Performance of Dances. When it came to the presentations, on the table with the diplomas there was a beautiful bowl of sweet peas, which my father had grown specially for the occasion. They really were a picture and Madam was thrilled to see all the different colours.

There were six graduates that year, including one male who had been a professional dancer but had decided to do the full three year course. He then joined Madame Espinosa at the London Studio Centre, as she needed a male teacher. The other five all took up teaching positions.

In the autumn term of 1981, Madam gave four lecture-demonstrations with the Teachers' Course and these were most challenging and informative for the students. They were to find out that she made great demands on her students and she insisted that they did want she wanted. I had told them about this, earlier, but now they were to experience it at first hand and they did not find it easy to deal with.

That year we started the new special One Year Course for ex-professional dancers. At first the special timetable was mainly Cecchetti, and under the direction of Richard Glasstone. The dancer taking this course was helped by the Resettlement Fund to do this.

Prior to this time the school had always used the crest of the Royal Opera House, but during this year, it was given its own crest, which included an eagle representing strength and a swan for grace. This meant that the Teachers' Training Course Diplomas had to be redesigned, with the crest at the centre top with gold leaf applied, and at the bottom right hand side, a red seal would be placed.

In May 1982 I made another visit to the Ballet School in Holland, just for one week. The school was running smoothly and fulfilling its purpose by feeding the companies with dancers. However, they still wanted me to return the following year. Once again, I wrote my report to the Minister of Arts.

Diploma Day proceeded as before, though we had to be content with the Sadler's Wells Studio because the company was in residence. Madam and Dame Alicia with the other guests watched the class I gave to the graduates prior to the Performance of Dances.

The reception was a truly special affair because the 1st and 2nd Years had a gift for the graduates, of a cake with the crest on the top. That was to be the start of another tradition, that the 1st and 2nd Years should give the graduates a cake. Those graduating gave me a most beautiful glass bowl with the crest engraved in the glass. One day this will go in the archives.

There were eleven graduates that year. Four of them were offered dancing contracts with companies in Europe, six were offered teaching positions, which included one at Elmhurst Ballet School and one went to study at the University in Nice, France. The ex-professional also received a diploma for his One Year Course.

After having two weeks family holiday on the Isle of Wight, my mother and I drove up to Yorkshire for a week, where I had been invited by David Gayle to teach at his Yorkshire Ballet Seminar. David had been the first boy on the original Craftsman's Course and was also a former dancer with The Royal Ballet Company and teacher at the school. He was founder and director of the Yorkshire Ballet Seminars which he started in 1973, to give students and teachers an opportunity of extending their knowledge and learning from top professional artists. Madam officially opened the first residential summer course at Ilkley College in 1975.

Dame Alicia Markova was a regular visiting lecturer during the five weeks course. With me were Moira Shearer, Pamela May and Alexis Rassine and we not only gave classes but talks as well, mine being a technical one. With the classes I never quite knew what the standard was going to be, until I had the students in front of me. The college was in a most beautiful setting on the edge of Ilkley Moor. David made sure that we were well taken care of and took us to some wonderful places for dinner.

For the next three years I accepted David's invitation. The following year, he started a two day Teachers' Course which Julia Farron conducted, and the following two years he asked me to take it. I must say I thoroughly enjoyed working with the teachers. It was so nice when Beryl Grey was with us because she always said that my mother reminded her of her own mother and they were able to have some lovely talks together.

In the autumn term of 1982, Sheelagh Lonergan, soloist with the Scottish Ballet Company, was given a years' leave of absence to attend the One Year Course, only this time it would be under the umbrella of the three year course. A special timetable was arranged around the one for the 3rd Years, and she took all the required examinations in order to receive the One Year Diploma for ex-professional dancers. This was to be the beginning of a number of ex-professionals doing the course in this way.

In October a memorial service was held at St. Paul's Church Covent Garden in gratitude for the work of Nora Roche, the Cecchetti teacher for the school over a period of many years, and the whole school attended.

During the Royal Academy of Dancing Special Week in January, the Imperial Group Genée Awards were held at the Palace Theatre, in London. We had such a lovely surprise when one of the 2nd Year students from the Teachers' Course who had entered won the Gold Medal. This gave the students on the course a tremendous uplift and encouragement to continue their hard work.

At Easter time that year, Donald McAlpine, the father of Louisa, who had graduated in 1978, invited me to give some ballet classes to students attending the special holiday course that he was holding at his dance school.

Early in May my father passed on and I was due to go to Holland in under two weeks time. It was decided that my mother and I would go together just for one week. The Ballet School had continued to progress and it was interesting to see them now well settled in their new building with five beautiful studios having all the most up-to-date equipment. Also, there was a theatre for the Ballet School to give performances. The Royal Ballet School in London was still sadly lacking all these advantages. At the end of my stay, I was thanked and told that my ten year assignment was up and that they would not need me any more. What ten year assignment? No one had ever told me!

Badges in the shape of the crest of The Royal Ballet School were ordered, with Dip RBS TTC. This would be something special just for the graduates to wear, and all had one, up to when I retired the first time in 1995. I happily wear mine, which was the master copy, each year at our Association Day.

Diploma Day 1983 proceeded as the previous year. The class and Performance of Dances and the presentations were held in the Sadler's Wells Studio, and the reception in the Baylis Hall. Dame

Alicia was there with other invited guests. This was to be the last year that James Monahan was to be with us, as he was retiring from the position of director of the school.

There were nine graduates that year, one of them wanting to have dancing experience first. The other eight were offered teaching positions and two of these were going to the Bush Davies School in East Grinstead. Sheelagh, who received the one Year Diploma, was returning to the Scottish Ballet to teach and direct the 'Steps Out' group attached to the company.

In the autumn term of 1983, Merle Park, a former ballerina with The Royal Ballet, became director of the school and soon after was made a Dame.

We decided to change the ruling with regard to the number of examinations needed to be passed in order to receive the diploma. I felt that we needed to keep our standard high, so in future it would be seven out of ten, instead of six.

Gilbert Mayer from the Paris Opera School came to give two weeks of master classes at the Upper School, and the Teachers' Course students were encouraged to watch whenever they could.

Graham Bowles, Head of Education, retired in the summer. He had taught me when I was a student and helped me so much at the beginning of the course regarding writing letters and various things I needed to know. He was always approachable and a charming person to have around and I knew I would miss him being there for me. His place was going to be taken by Nigel Grant.

Jean Bedells was also retiring from teaching the RAD Major Syllabus and wished to give an award on Diploma Day, to 'the graduate with the best RAD teaching examination results', and who would be taking up a teaching position. The award was the book *Theatre Street* by Tamara Karsavina.

On Diploma Day 1984 we were able to have the Covent Garden Studio, which was always appreciated because it gave us more space. The class was now turning into a Demonstration Class. This was followed by the Performance of Dances which we videoed for the first time. The reception was held in the Sadler's Wells Studio which also gave us more room.

There were eight graduates that year. One of them wanted to further her studies at the London Studio Centre, two were offered dancing contracts and five were offered teaching positions. The one ex-professional attending the One Year Course was also offered a teaching position in Hong Kong.

In the autumn term of 1984 I found myself without an assistant. Because the numbers in the Upper School had been reduced it meant that the class Hope had been responsible for on the Dancers' Course no longer existed and the school could not keep her on as a full-time member of staff. I was absolutely devastated, because I knew the amount of work that had to be done running a Teachers' Course, which was quite different from the Dancers' Course, as I had to sit in on all the examinations during the year and conduct all the private interviews needed to help them achieve their goal. I was told I could ask help from the 3rd Years, but I knew how busy they were and that arrangement would not work. Also, I only had the help of a part-time secretary.

There were a number of timetable changes. Hope, now a freelance teacher in and around London at various schools, would take over the RAD Grade Syllabus and continue with the two other RAD classes which she taught. Denise Winmill, since graduating, had become an RAD Major Examiner and would take over all the Major Syllabus classes which Jean Bedells had taught before retiring. Karen Greenhead was now the teacher for Dalcroze Eurythmics.

During the past year we had had two ex-professionals, one from Sweden and the other from Holland. They had wanted to do the full Three Year Course, but were both informed by their countries that they could only receive money for one more year. Hearing that, I had to work out a special programme for each, so that they could complete the syllabus in two years and receive an ex-professional Two Year Diploma.

Diploma Day 1985. Great excitement! For the first time we were able to use the newly built Arnold Haskell Theatre Studio at Barons Court which had raised seating that could be pulled out or stacked away as required. There were curtains and all the equipment necessary for lighting. Madam said that the former graduates should now come and watch those graduating in their Demonstration Class. This gave a special feeling to the day because of their support.

Over the years, I had been developing quite a challenging set of exercises, stamina wise, at the barre, and I would from then on repeat this every year so that those graduates watching knew what the difficulties were, and applauded at the appropriate time in order

to give some breathing space. All the exercises choreographed for the centre were freshly arranged each year to suit the particular group. The final ending to the class was always kept the same, and was to a beautiful piece of music which Tom Young had written. It really did cause a tear to flow when I taught it to the graduates each year.

Barbara Fewster made the remark that the class looked like a corps de ballet and I replied that that is what they should look like, even if they are on the Teachers' Course. After the Performance of Dances, the audience were offered soft drinks, while we set the stage for the presentations. To add to the awards, Dr Backhouse was now giving a prize to the graduate with the best Anatomy results. The reception was again held in the Baylis Hall.

There were nine graduates that year. Seven of them were offered dancing contracts and two had teaching positions to go to. The professional from Holland returned to teach at the Koninklijk Conservatorium at The Hague, and the other one from Sweden returned to Gothenburg where she was to dance and teach. That year we had also had a ex-professional taking the One Year Course, and she was going to be teaching in London.

That summer of 1985 had marked twenty years of Madam presenting diplomas, and we now had one hundred and fifty eight graduates around the world, in the United States, Canada, Cayman Islands, Australia, New Zealand, Japan, Thailand, Hong Kong, Malaysia, Singapore, Nepal, South Africa, Saudi Arabia, Canary Islands, France, Germany, Sweden, Belgium, Austria, Italy, Netherlands, Norway, Greece, Luxembourg, Guernsey, Scotland, and Wales, and all across England.

Soon after my father retired in 1972, he had suggested that I should have two maps, one of the world and one of the British Isles, so that I could place a flag in all the places where the graduates were teaching. He made these up for me and stuck them onto hardboard and they stayed until I retired. I had these maps placed on the walls on either side of my desk in my office. I think they made quite an impression on visitors, and they went on to be quite full of flags as the graduates continued to grow in number.

Chapter 14

Working up to my retirement

It was clear that 1985 was going to be another exciting year! The 3rd Years were a lovely group to work with and were already doing their best, like the previous year's group, to help me as much as possible, knowing full well that I did not have Hope to assist me.

In the autumn term, Pamela May started to teach mime scenes to the 1st Years, after they had learnt all the vocabulary with me. Vivienne Saxton was on a leave of absence for one year in America, and Robert Harrold, an ISTD Examiner, taught her classes for us. Madam now said that the 3rd Years should be allowed to join the Dancers' Course classes by rota four days in the week. I was pleased about this, firstly because Madam recognised that their standard of work would be acceptable for the teacher concerned and because it also reduced my class number by two.

On the 5th and 6th of March we were due for another visit by the Department of Education and Science in order to receive our accreditation. As I was taking the team around, they said to me, 'you do not need to take us, your assistant can do it!' That was my opportunity to tell them that I did not have one. Their reply was that it was imperative that I should have one and that they would include this in their report. Apart from that, everything was excellent.

With regard to having an assistant, my mother came up with the suggestion that I should keep one of the graduating students for a year. That would not only help me but would also be something special that the student concerned could put on her CV. The important advantage for the school, which might make it possible, was that it would not cost them as much as someone on a full-time salary. I took this suggestion to the school, and after some discussion, it was accepted with the proviso that I took two more students onto the course.

The Royal Ballet School needed to have an embosser for the seals on the diplomas and their other official papers. I was asked to go and deal with purchasing one. When thinking about it, it became clear that just having the lettering around the edge was not sufficient, as the centre of the circle looked bare. My mother came up with the idea of having the small crown from the top of the crest on the diplomas put in the centre. I remember seeing her tracing it onto a piece of grease-proof paper. When I took the suggestion to the school, they were very happy with the idea, and I was then able to go ahead and place the order. My mother really did come in very useful at times over a variety of issues; she seemed to be able to see things so clearly from an outside perspective.

Diploma Day, 1986, was our 21st anniversary of presenting diplomas. It was just so wonderful that we had the use of the Arnold Haskell Theatre Studio for this now very special occasion in our calendar of events. The audience, having grown over the years, now practically filled the theatre. The specially invited guests included Anthony Dowell and Peter Wright, the two Royal Ballet company directors. We were also able to video the whole proceedings for the first time in order to have a record.

The Demonstration Class and Performance of Dances went very well, and Tom Young played some beautiful music. He was always such a strong support to me.

When it came to the presentations, Julia Ellis, who was the head student that year, gave a very good speech, and it confirmed my decision that she was the right one to be my assistant for the forthcoming year, a fact which I was very happy to publicly announce at that time.

As I always did, I asked Madam if she would like to speak and she replied

'I have just been asked if I would like to say something, and it is rather well known you cannot stop me. I do want to place on re- cord and to thank the friend on my right for the excellent dancing and performance I have just witnessed. It was excellent dancing, very careful and well constructed with knowledge behind it. I am going to pick out one thing which made a great impression on me, and it is everyone's ports de bras. I have not seen two arms in the air so carefully placed and considered for a long time... I saw the most perfect *ports de bras* today in every group, and if you are going to teach children, that is basic, like walking on a tightrope to keep the perfect balance.'

She then went on to wish them all the very best, either dancing or teaching, and to say that she hoped they had enjoyed the day as much as she had.

What praise to come from Madam! I was so grateful that she had seen one of the things that I have always worked on so hard with my students, remembering my days at the school when I was told that my arm movements were terrible, and that I should go and watch Beryl Grey and Svetlana Beriosova. My arms were very long and most of my teachers had short arms which just naturally fell into the right shape.

There were twelve graduates that year. One of them wished to do further studies to gain an M.A. in Dance at London University; another was offered a teaching position at London Studio Centre; seven were auditioning for a dancing contract. Another was returning to Athens to dance and teach, and yet another had a contract to dance in Spain. Of course, there was also Julia Ellis, who was going to be my assistant for the next year.

Coming back for the autumn term of 1986, how wonderful it was to have help again after two years of having to somehow survive. Julia had a desk in my office and soon gained a feel of the way things worked, I could confidently trust her to do what I asked.

We had three ex-professionals doing the One Year Course, so that meant three individual timetables for them. Amanda Maxwell was from London Festival Ballet, Jill Porter from Dublin City Ballet and Ruth Prior from Scottish Ballet. They were a responsible group and settled well into the way of being a student again. That is not always the case for ex-professionals, who often find it hard to work as a student again and to being open to receiving correction. Years later, Amanda became responsible for teaching all the Character work at the Upper School.

On Sunday the 7th of December there was a Dance for Africa Appeal at the school, and with the other members of staff, I gave classes to anyone who paid the minimum of £3. This included the members of the Fire Service at Hammersmith and just anyone who wanted to come. The Teachers' Course and Dancers' Course all joined in with these classes too.

In the summer term, the course was awarded the 'Isabel Haxell Cup' by the National Dance Branch for the furtherance of the National Work. Candidates from the course had been entered for examinations for the past twenty-three years. I was asked to go and collect the cup on behalf of the course, during the Summer Congress.

Diploma Day 1987, was the first time that Madam had been unable to be with us. Her husband was very ill and she said she could not leave him. She had, however, telephoned Dame Alicia who had been attending for a number of years and asked her if she would kindly do the honours, so we were very grateful to her for standing in, and giving her valuable thoughts on teaching.

The whole day went as on previous occasions and it was greatly enjoyed by all. There were five graduates that year, plus the three ex-professionals. One was offered a soloist contract with the company in Kiel, another went to teach for Julia Barry, a former graduate, at her school in New Zealand; and three wanted to have stage experience. The remaining three all had teaching positions to go to.

As there did not seem to be the right person to take Julia's place as my assistant for the forthcoming year, I asked if she would like to stay for another year, which she seemed very happy to do. This was wonderful for me, because by now she knew how the ship was run.

Returning for the autumn term in 1987, there were only a few changes to the timetable, except for the fact that Julia Ellis was able to take over and teach all the Cecchetti classes, while Jocelyn Mather was away on a year's leave of absence. During this time Julia had excellent examination results with the students. Norman Morrice took over the choreographic workshop for the 3rd Years from Richard Glasstone.

This year we had one ex-professional on the One Year Course, Anthony Sewell, who had been dancing with a company in Germany, and we arranged a special timetable for him.

On Thursday the 8th of October, Princess Diana visited the school and the company. The 3rd Years put on a display of Spanish dancing which she enjoyed, and she was very keen for me to tell her all about the graduates and the various positions they took up after graduating, either dancing or teaching. After being with us, she went across to the Covent Garden Studio to see the company, but before leaving she said, 'I will be back because I would like to see some more.' So while she was away, we gathered ourselves together, and true to her word, she did come back and sit down again. It was such a privilege for me to have this very relaxed and informal talk with her. What a joy for us all!

During the year, the RAD brought out their registration scheme. All the names of past Diploma graduates were sent to the RAD, so that each one could write and apply for provisional registration if they were teaching and were expecting to send pupils in for examinations. From now on, no pupils could take examinations unless their teacher was registered.

On Diploma Day that year, I opened the presentations by extending our sincere congratulations to Madam on her 90th year and expressing our gratitude for all the help and encouragement she had given to the course since she started it 25 years ago.

At that occasion I also paid tribute to Barbara Fewster, who was retiring. We had been friends over many years, coming from the same school in Bournemouth, and had worked so happily together. I thanked her for her devoted years to the school and for passing on all her valuable knowledge to the course.

I was also able to announce that Caroline Barrett, who had been the head student, would take over from Julia as my assistant for the forthcoming year. Out of the ten graduating, eight had been offered teaching positions either here or abroad and the other two wanted to have stage experience.

In September, there were not really any changes to the timetable and Caroline soon settled down and proved her organising skills. The arrangement turned out to be another good choice. She was also asked to teach Dance Studies at White Lodge.

We had two dancers over from La Scala, Milan. They had been given leave of absence from the company to study Benesh Notation at the Institute and wanted to take classes with our students, so a special timetable was arranged for them. We also had an ex-professional from Denmark wanting to do the One Year Course, so a timetable was made for her.

In February a memorial service was held for Michael Wood, our previous director, in the Guards Chapel at Wellington Barracks. That was an occasion not to be forgotten.

On Sunday the 23rd of April, the Teachers' Course started The Royal Ballet School 'Buy A Brick Appeal', I gave a Demonstration Class in front of as many parents, family and friends as we could invite, all paying £5 for entry. Towards the end of the class, we concentrated on raising any extra money we could. Three of the students said they would attempt thirty-two *fouettés*, and they did.

It was 5p a *fouetté*. Two more students attempted fifteen *entrechat six* for the same amount, and they made it. Another did six *entrechat six de volé*. We were pleased because we raised nearly £1,000 and one of our ex-graduates also raised £1,000 at her own ballet school for the appeal.

Diploma Day 1989 was now able to follow the usual pattern, the one exception being an award for 'Excellence in Benesh Notation', which went to Mondy from Thailand. She happened to be the niece of the first student that we had from Thailand.

Madam said:

'As usual, I am very happy to be here again, and congratulate everyone on the results of this morning. There is one thing that particularly excited me, and that was the musicality of them all. I have never seen better phrasing of arms in relation to head, which is so important when teaching and to know how to pass it on to pupils.'

I was able to announce that Dimitra Kouremeti from Greece would be my assistant for the forthcoming year. Caroline was going to be married to Anthony from the previous year and they had both been offered teaching positions at the Hammond School in Chester. Three of the graduates were wanting to dance and have stage experience and the other five had been offered teaching positions. Some would be travelling abroad and others would be in this country.

Caroline and Anthony had a lovely wedding in Bournemouth, which my mother and I were invited to attend.

In September we returned for the autumn term 1989, with Dimitra taking on the job of assisting me. She was always very enthusiastic and soon became familiar with what was needed. Our only change to the timetable was that Mary Miller, the actress, took over all the voice production lessons and we were very grateful to have her.

That term we had five ex-professional dancers to take the One Year Course. One from Sadler's Wells Royal Ballet, one from La Scala, one from the Kirov, and two from the commercial theatre. Most of the time they followed a special timetable. Unfortunately one left after one term.

On the 20th of May we had the first 'In House Day,' which was to become a yearly event. It was to give parents and friends an opportunity to see the students at work. The success of the 'Buy a

Brick Day,' when all parents were invited, had started this off. I gave a classical class to the 2nd and 3rd Years, with John McCarthy at the piano. The 1st Years then showed a character demonstration given by Maria Fay, with Fred Loftin playing.

Towards the end of June, I heard that I had two cancellations for the forthcoming autumn term, because these students were unable to receive a grant. I was told that unless I could replace these students with two more, even though it was so late in the term, I would not be able to have an assistant.

I really had to really think deeply about this, and it suddenly came to me, what makes two? Twins! I remembered having seen twins sometime during the year, but had no idea when or where. It took two days for the secretary to find the papers and the twins were from Wales. It turned out that the mother was a dancing teacher but whether she was theirs or not I did not know, because the name was different and my notes on their previous audition were not all that promising.

The papers came onto my desk about 4.15 p.m. I took one look and decided to wait until the next day before calling, and then suddenly changed my mind and felt it was right to telephone straight away. The mother answered the telephone and I asked if she was their dancing teacher, to which she replied 'yes.' My next question to her was, 'how keen are your daughters to teach?' The answer was very definite, that was all they both wanted to do and had spent the previous weekend watching classes at White Lodge. They both helped their mother whenever they could. All this gave me the feeling that I should offer them both a place and review the situation at the end of the year.

I then said, 'and how would you feel if I offered your daughters a place for the coming year?' Her answer was, 'without a final audition?' My reply was 'Yes.' 'Well,' she said, 'we will have to apply for grants, it will not be possible without.' She then said she would apply the next day and call me back. She added that when I called, they were just going out of the front door to talk to their headmistress about what they would be studying the following year. How right it was to have called when I did!

The next day I received a telephone call from the joyful mother to say that because her daughters were twins, the grant authorities were prepared to give them both a grant for the full three years. This really was a miracle, because the money had already been allotted by the end of May.

These two girls worked so hard that they were able to raise their standard of classical ballet to a good level and both gained the diploma. The joy on Diploma Day was to see them both dancing the two Red Girls from the ballet *Les Patineurs* and they did it so well. What a wonderful story, and I was able to keep my much-needed assistant.

Diploma Day was on the 6th of July 1990. Our invited guests that year included Monica Mason, Anthony Dowell, Anne Heaton and John Field. Another landmark would be passed as we would be giving out the two hundredth diploma.

Madam's speech again was most complimentary, and she spoke as follows:

> 'I think I can safely say that the performance this year has been an outstanding one – I don't remember a better one. In fact, it is the best I have ever seen, and I thoroughly enjoyed it and have seen some lovely dancing.
>
> Time and time again I have praised the musicality of these dancers, and today I found I was accepting that as a matter of course, and my interest was turned to another line in their approach. I am speaking as an ex-student of the London School of Art where I studied for a year between the ages of 16 and 17 years from 9 a.m. until 2 p.m. in the afternoon in what they called the Antique Class, which was devoted to what I was admiring today – 'Line', 'Proportion', 'Dimension'. I find these girls are extremely sensitive to the importance of this in everything they do. If any of them are going to be budding choreographers, I congratulate them because nothing is more helpful than to know something about 'Line'. That experience came back to me as I was sitting here this morning – the outline of the whole drawing – I felt this very strongly through their classwork and the execution of the very lovely dances.
>
> I want to thank them all and to congratulate them on a really exciting morning, and to congratulate the lady on my right for the very important part she played.'

That year we had eight graduates from the Three Year Course. One had been offered a soloist contract with a company in Germany. Another was going to further her studies at the Vaganova School in Leningrad and six had been offered teaching positions. These included Clare Howarth, who had been the head student, and I was able to announce that I was offering her the job of assisting me for the forthcoming year. Three of the ex-professionals received a diploma and all had been offered teaching positions. The one remaining received a certificate of completion.

In September 1990, it was a joy to have Clare helping me, as she was so cool, calm, and collected, and seemed able to take on responsibility easily. She also took on the duty of being Assistant Warden at Wolf House, where a number of students from the Dancers' Course and Teachers' Course lived. She was also living there herself.

We had three ex-professionals join us for that year to take the One Year Course. One was from the Covent Garden Opera Ballet, another from a company in Singapore and one from the Istanbul Ballet Company. Fortunately, there were very few changes to the timetable.

Apart from the now yearly event of the 'In House Day,' when parents and friends came to visit during the month of May, that year passed off as one of the quietest on record. We were just able to take things in our stride without too many interruptions.

On Diploma Day in July 1991 we celebrated the 25th anniversary of presenting diplomas. Everything followed the same pattern as on previous years, except that the original group who graduated in 1966 wished to give an award. It was a silver bowl, which they wanted to give to the student who had shown the most 'Strength and Grace' throughout their three years on the course. That meant that we now had six awards to present. When I asked Madam if she would like to speak, this was her reply:

> 'Miss Adams has just asked me if I want to say something. I think I have never so much wanted to say something as I have this year. They are celebrating 25 years of this little organisation, which is marvellous work, not only here but abroad. What is unique about it, it is celebrating 25 years under the same director. Valerie Adams took on the challenge 25 years ago. She was young, and what she has achieved and done you know, and I only have to remind you, and for us to give her a vote of thanks.'

For me to hear this from Madam was most moving and I was so grateful.

There were eight graduates from the Three Year Course that year, and three ex-professionals, and they had all been offered teaching positions. I was happy to be able to announce that Teresa Hallam, the head student, would be my assistant for the forthcoming year.

In the autumn term of 1991 I was glad to find that yet again I had another good organiser in Teresa, and she also had taken on the same responsibilities as Clare at Wolf House.

That year, we had two ex-professionals join us, one from the Dublin Contemporary Company and a Japanese lady from the Christchurch Ballet Company in New Zealand.

There were only two changes to the timetable; Tom Young would take over all the Music classes, and in the spring term Mary Goodhew, who had graduated from the One Year Course two years previously, took over all the Cecchetti classes from Jocelyn Mather.

In February, we were again due for a visit from the accreditation committee. It was always quite a tense time during their two days visit, but we need not have worried because as usual the outcome was excellent.

The Youth Ballet Workshop under the direction of Jill Tookey asked us for helpers to assist with their auditions, rehearsals, and performances, and twelve of our students gave their assistance. This was all wonderful experience for them and this practice has continued over the years.

In May we had the usual 'In House Day' for parents and friends to visit. This occasion always seemed to be much appreciated by all.

Diploma Day 1992 proceeded as in previous years, and during the Programme of Dances, we were able to see for the last time Tina Chen dancing one of her beautiful Chinese dances. For the three years she had been on the course, we had been treated to one of these each year.

After the presentations, as I usually did, I asked Madam if she would like to say a few words, and her reply was as follows.

'Of course I would like to, I would just like to let you know, how as usual I have loved the dancing. I love the discipline, and I loved the choreography of the dances, and really carefully worked out execution.

If you can get a student to think as carefully, then when she teaches they will do it too. This is what I like about this Teachers' Training

Course, you have got to be able to do it yourself. Do it yourself and then pass it on to your pupils.

A lovely afternoon, delightful dancing, excellent interpretation and I was also keen on the musicality, which is so important for teachers to understand. I wish them all the very best and hope you have enjoyed the afternoon as much as I have.'

There were nine graduates that year plus the two ex-professionals. Three were going to be dancing as well as teaching and the rest teaching. Besides this country, they were going to Australia, Canada, Japan, Singapore, Cyprus and France.

Tina Chen, one of the graduates from the Three Year Course, had during the past year gained her RAD Solo Seal. She was the first student from the course to do so. It had been such a pleasure to coach her for this and to have had her on the course. She was so receptive to everything she was told and it reminded me of when I was in the school and Miss Edwards would say to us, 'don't come back tomorrow unless you can do it'.

On the 12th of July Tina gave a performance at the Bloomsbury Theatre in London. She not only danced but also played the piano. She showed a variety of dances from different countries and only had a musician to help when she had a quick change. She donated £500 from the proceeds to the de Valois fund to help graduates with their travel, if they wished to come for a refresher course.

Following this, Tina gave a series of sixteen performances in London, Hong Kong, Singapore, and Taiwan, before returning to this country to do an M.A. Dance Study Course at Surrey University. Together with her husband, she is now director of a large purpose-built dance school in Shanghai, China.

In the autumn term, 1992, I had Teresa to help me again for another year, which she was happy to do. Like all the other graduates, I had chosen to help me in the past, she proved to be so efficient and well organised and gracious in the way she handled things, which was so wonderful to see and experience.

We had two ex-professional dancers joining us that year for the One Year Course. One was from Hong Kong, and the other from Japan.

Towards the end of November the Royal Opera House held a Study Day called 'Dance into the Future'. Students from the Teachers' Course were invited to show a ballet class and as I felt Teresa was capable of teaching this class, I asked her to stand in for me.

In December and January The Royal Ballet were giving fifteen performances of the ballet *Tales of Beatrix Potter* at the Royal Opera House, and one 3rd Year student was needed to help at each performance. A really lovely experience for them to be so involved.

In January I received my Fellowship from the Royal Academy of Dancing for exceptional service to the Academy. It was held at the Queen Elizabeth Hall, and there were just three of us that year. My seat was on the end of the row and during the interval a lady came and sat on the step at the side of me and said, 'do you remember me from Holland?' How could I forget! She was the student who had made it necessary for me to run a Teachers' Course there. She was visiting London for the first time and was so thrilled to be there when I received my Fellowship.

In the new year, a Teachers' Training Course Committee of Enquiry, consisting of eight members, was formed to discuss the possible options for the future of the course after my retirement in July 1995. I was not included. The findings would be reviewed by the Board of Governors in March 1993.

In May we had the usual 'In House Day,' and the following week we held a 'Teachers' Day,' when former teachers of the students were invited to come and watch classes throughout the day. A special timetable was arranged for this occasion.

As in previous years, the students from the course were needed to help with the school performance at the Royal Opera House and for the performances at Holland Park.

Earlier in the summer, Madam had been in hospital and when she was recovering in a nursing home in Wimbledon, I went to see her. This was certainly not the first time, because over the years since she had been devoting more of her time to the school, I had often been asked to take things to her that she needed, mail and notepaper etc. This time she said she would certainly do her utmost to attend Diploma Day as she wanted to be there. She had always said that it was one of the happiest days in her calendar each year.

Diploma Day 1993 arrived and we still did not know if Madam would be able to attend. As had been the case for a number of years, I asked David Gayle if he would kindly pick her up in his car. In the Programme of Dances that year, we had included the Black Queen solo from Madam's ballet *Checkmate*. Danella Bedford was dancing it as a tribute to Madam and naturally I hoped that she would see it. It was the last but one item on the programme and just as I was about to announce it, Madam walked in. We naturally paused to allow her to take her seat before continuing. I then announced the solo, and will always remember I did it with such a positive tone and with such gratitude that Madam was actually there to see Danella give such a good performance.

In spite of things not being easy for her, Madam did stay and present the diplomas with her usual smile for each and all the graduates. It reminded me of another time some years before, when there was a difficulty and she said 'I have to present the diplomas first, before I leave.' She always seemed to have a clear sense of priorities, whatever the occasion

Madam did speak at this occasion and said,

'I wonder if you will forgive me with a broken leg, for not trying to stand up. I do appreciate having you all being here again this year. If you have an ambition in your heart, you should follow it, and not only think of strong feet and big jumps, but we need to look into our hearts and see if there is another ambition hidden away and make sure we follow that.'

She then said that she was the best dancer in her class, and when the teacher had left at the end of the class, she liked to rearrange all the steps in a different way. That of course was the beginning of her interest in choreography.

There were eleven graduates from the Three Year Course and two ex-professionals leaving us that year. One had a contract to dance and teach in Sweden. Another had a contract to be the Benesh Choreologist for the Hamburg Ballet Company. Yet another had a contract to dance in the USA and the other eight had teaching positions to go to. I was happy to be able to announce that Danella Bedford, who had been the head student, had been asked to be my assistant for the forthcoming year. Teresa was going to take up a teaching position in New Zealand.

Later in July I was invited by Ross Alley to give a classical ballet class at the seminar he was holding in London. The title he wanted me to work on and explain was 'Bringing Adage to Life'. This was something that I felt strongly about, so it was an enjoyable thing to do. He actually invited me again the next year and the title was

'Encouraging Life and Feeling in Movement,' again something that I felt was so important.

That month, an advertisement was sent out worldwide in search of a principal for the new Teachers' Course.

In September, 1993, we had four ex-professional dancers join us for the One Year Course. Graham Fletcher from The Royal Ballet and commercial theatre, Li Jiong from China, Hiroko Nishikawa and Kafuyu Shintani, both from Japan.

The timetable changes included Cara Drower taking over all the Cecchetti classes and Anna Meadmore the 'A' Level Dance classes for the 1st Year.

During that term I wrote an article about my career for The Royal Ballet School *Sidelines*, and in the following March the *Dancing Times* published an article about my career, written by Sue Merrett.

In the new year, Alison Hayward, who had been chosen as my successor, took up her position as Principal Designate, to give her plenty of time to settle in.

The 'In House Day' in May for parents and friends took place as usual, but after watching the Classical Class and Character Demonstration, we also showed some solos and the 3rd Years danced the Spanish ' Farrouca' and 'Jota'.

As usual, all the students on the course were involved, helping with the school performance at the Royal Opera House and with the performances at Holland Park.

Diploma Day in July 1994 was again another exciting day and planned as in previous years. During the Performances of Dances, Li Jiong danced a most beautiful solo of *The Dying Swan* and Kafuyu showed a traditional Japanese dance. Through the years, it had been such a treat for us to see the ex-professionals share their experience as dancers at this occasion, and for us to see the traditional dances of their countries performed by those from abroad.

After the presentations, Madam said that,

'It has been a lovely time as usual, and I love to be with you. Thank you so much for remembering to ask me. It is just one of those highlights of the dancing years.'

There were eight graduates from the Three Year Course that year. One had been offered a dancing contract with 'Bluebells' in France, another had a modelling contract and the rest were offered teaching positions. The ex-professionals were also offered teaching positions.

Danella, who had been a truly excellent assistant during the past year, was taking up a teaching position in Charlotte, USA. I was unable to announce my assistant for the forthcoming year, as I would have to share with Alison the person she would be choosing to be her course co-ordinator.

The next year was not an easy one for me, without having my own assistant. There were so many things to organise and have ready for the takeover. On one of my visits to see Madam, she said she would try and hold on until I retired. What a wonderful thing for her to say!

In January 1995 I was invited by the Royal Academy of Dancing to give a lecture-demonstration at the Queen Elizabeth Hall, entitled 'Relating Movement to Music Through *Enchaînements*'. I used my students from the 2nd and 3rd Years, and was able to have my pianist Thomas McLelland-Young, with whom I had worked for so many years. We arranged a very interesting session in which he spoke about things from his own point of view as a pianist and how he could help the dancers with the way he was playing. He also contributed greatly by his explanations of the different pieces of music involved.

I tried to explain how the music and movement had to blend, and how one had to feel the rhythm and beat, and that it had to become an integral part of one's being. For something to have feeling, life, and expression, there has to be breathing – and to have that, there has to be a pulse, a heart beat, which must be regular and rhythmical. Something that is alive has to have all this, plus an eye focus, which naturally gives balance. One interpretation of inspiration is to breathe into – so for us to see or give an inspiring performance, all this has to take place.

The next important thing is that when one is listening to music, it is necessary to discipline oneself to hear the dynamics that are going on – the depth, breadth, height, in other words, what goes up, down, and around. It is then amazing to see how wonderfully the *enchaînements* begin to unfold in front of one's eyes, so to speak.

In May we had the usual 'In House Day,' and as in previous years, we showed a variety of dances after the classes.

By now, I realised that I needed more help in preparing for Diploma Day. It really had to be someone who had been there before and knew what was required and could take responsibility. I knew that Danella was the one to call on to assist me. She was coming over to teach *Kaleidoscope* a very successful piece she had choreographed for a previous year. I called her in America, to ask if she could come over a week sooner to help me, which she happily agreed to do.

By the end of June all the examinations had been completed and it was known that all eight graduates from the Three Year Course and the one ex-professional would be receiving their diplomas.

Out of the eight graduates that year, three wanted to continue their studies, at the Rambert School, the Benesh Institute, and London Studio Centre. Two were offered dancing contracts in America and Germany and the other three were offered teaching positions, one of them returning to her home country, New Zealand. The ex-professional was also negotiating for a teaching position there too.

We then had just two weeks to prepare for my final Diploma Day, and Danella had arrived. As the celebrations were to be extended because of my retirement, I had to make the Demonstration Class shorter in length, and to swell the numbers I asked three of the 2nd Years, Mikah Smillie, Eliza Tang and Anna Atkinson, to join the eight graduates. Tom Young would naturally be playing for us.

The Programme of Dances would then follow, though this year with only eight items instead of the usual twelve. As this was a special year, I asked a number of the ex-graduates to choreograph some of the dances. Tania Fairbairn choreographed a Russian dance for five, which would open the programme, then we continued with *Tanguillo,* one of Ana Ricarda's special dances, which would be danced by three of the graduates. The third item was a *Demi-Caractère Solo,* which Philip Pegler had choreographed as one of the requirements of the course.

The fourth piece, entitled *For You Who Goes, From Us Who Stay, With Thanks* was choreographed by Julia Ellis. She arrived from Switzerland to arrange this Classical piece, and I remember her asking me how many dancers she would have. At that moment, I could not tell her, as only having seven girls, it was difficult to arrange the programme. As it happened, she started off with four and was joined by another two after a very quick change, and it turned out to be a most beautiful piece. She, like Danella, certainly had a gift for choreography. The fifth item on the programme would be a solo from the ballet *Don Quixote,* danced by Katherine Wood. The sixth item, would be a *Pas de Deux* called *Autumn,* choreographed by James Supervia, who was the ex-professional on the course that year. He arranged it for Mikah Smillie from the 2nd Year and Philip Pegler; it was a truly lovely piece, to music by Glazunov. This proved that James, too, had a gift for choreography.

The seventh item was going to be a *Tribute to Madam* a traditional Irish dance, arranged by Vivienne Saxton to the music from *Riverdance* by Bill Whelan. We needed some material to make the costumes and Danella was brilliant, taking complete responsibility. She went to a market in Kensington High Street and not only found suitable material but also a lady there who agreed to make the costumes for us more or less overnight. We had been promised that we could borrow five black cloaks from the company wardrobe at the Royal Opera House. That turned out to be a story too long to explain here, but happily we were able to have them in the end.

To finish the programme, we were closing with Danella's *Kaleidoscope*, and as before, I knew it would be a great success.

The school performance that year, always held at the Royal Opera House, took place the day before our big day on the Saturday. The programme consisted of *Valse fantaisie*, *Peter and the Wolf* and *The Two Pigeons*. In the main programme, an article was printed called 'A Dedicated Life.' This was all about my career, and also had a photograph of my teaching. I was grateful that this gesture had been made.

Diploma Day on Sunday the 16th of July 1995 had arrived, and that morning I realised that we would be celebrating thirty years of Madam presenting diplomas. That year, it was to be held at the Margot Fonteyn Theatre in Richmond Park, attached to the The Royal Ballet Lower School, as we were expecting many more guests and ex-graduates from all over the world to attend. These included Sir Anthony Dowell and Sir Peter Wright, the two directors of the Royal Ballet Companies, and other distinguished guests from the ballet world.

At 1.30 p.m., John Mitchell, the academic principal at White Lodge, welcomed everyone and said that afterwards, during tea, I wanted to speak to as many ex-graduates as possible. He just mentioned that 'the park gates closed at 9 p.m.,' at which everyone laughed.

We then started with the Demonstration Class, and the Performance of Dances, which both went really well. While the graduates prepared themselves for the presentations, the guests were given refreshments and walked around the gardens.

The graduates now ready, we were able to proceed with the Presentation Ceremony and after Madam had presented the diplomas and all the awards, I asked her if she would like to say a few words. At the age of ninety-seven, she spoke with a clear voice and no microphone as follows:

> 'Needless to say, I am terribly happy to be here again with you all, at this lovely hall. I love this part of the world – it seems to be the root of everything we have ever done, and I hope it remains so forever, – and it will of course with all your support.
>
> A very special and lovely occasion. Lovely in the sense of happy memories, and sad in a sense it has come to this point. Valerie has done a job for us, well, I don't know how to talk about it. You know what it was like when she started, not like this:– it was pretty 'muggy', shall we say – she never ever fluffed anything, however deep the mud, however difficult, Valerie was always there doing her utmost, and I speak from my heart when I tell you, she is one of my oldest and dearest friends and members of staff the school has ever had – I speak from my heart, and when I have done this there is little more to say.'

To hear what Madam had just said was really so moving and I felt very grateful that she had been able to be there, and my mother too. This was followed by Philip Pegler as head student giving his speech, which was excellent.

It was then my turn! First of all I thanked everyone for coming, and especially all the graduates who had travelled from eleven countries and all across Europe and the British Isles to be with me on that very special occasion and to support those graduating. There were in fact around one hundred and seventy-five, out of two hundred and sixty-four ex-graduates who were present.

I gave thanks to all the teachers and pianists who had been involved with the course, and said that 'coming from a naval family, I knew that a ship had to have a captain, but that it is working together as a team with the crew that makes for plain sailing. I had been fortunate to have a team who had given of their very best to make this course the success it had been.' At that point, we gave gifts to all the members of staff who were now leaving. In fact a number of them had stayed on until I retired, which was very kind of them.

I continued, 'this really is a day of giving thanks. My career has been a challenge all the way and I am grateful to have made it to this day. There had been a number of times when I had felt it was impossible to continue. The workload of teaching and running the course often seemed too much and it was only possible through the support and encouragement of my mother and of kind friends, past and present, who had helped and guided me to see things in their true light, so that I could handle the situations as they came along. All I ever wanted to do was to teach! The office work had grown out of all proportion.'

I then thanked Barbara Fewster and Graham Bowles, with whom I had worked for so long, and continued: 'but it was to Madam, that I owed so much. My goal as a little girl was to join the Sadler's Wells Company. Madam accepted me into the school where she was one of my teachers and then gave me the opportunity to join the company at Covent Garden. When I felt teaching was to be my career, Madam was the one who said she would train me at the school. After being on the staff at the school and then spending over five years in Holland, I returned to be on the full-time staff again. It was then that Madam asked me if I would be interested to be at her side when she formed the Teachers' Course. The rest is history, and I was so grateful to her, for having had the confidence and trust to place the course in my hands and give me such a rewarding career.'

I then gave Alison some flowers and handed over the course, wishing her all the very best.

It was now time for the last part of this very special day for me – a tribute would take the form of 'This is Your Life.' It had all been masterminded and arranged by Alison and her team, Hope, Vivienne, and Denise. I knew absolutely nothing about it. It had been kept a complete secret.

I was asked to wait in the wings, while the curtain went up on a stage strung with flags across the air, stretching from one side to the other, which the 1st Years had painted. These were of all the countries where the graduates were working. Seated at a table were Madam, Dame Merle Park, and my mother, who had been persuaded to be there too and be part of the tribute. My mother told me later that when Madam saw her, she said, 'who are you?' A couple of years before when I was visiting Madam, she had asked me how old my mother was. After her insisting that I tell her, she said, 'oh, but she is a mere chicken!' Now, confronted with the question, my mother replied, 'you called me a chicken!' Madam then said, 'oh, you are Valerie's mother!' How sharp that was, from both of them! I was then called by Alison to take the seat at the side of Madam.

Alison then spoke about my early days, before calling on the guest speakers: Elizabeth Collins, one of my first teachers in Bournemouth; then Pamela May, from our days together in the company and teaching at the school; Lynn Wallis, one of my former pupils on the Dancers' Course at the school, and a teacher; Hope Keelan, one of my former students on the course and my assistant of nine years; Tom Young, the wonderful pianist I had shared so many classes with and who was playing that day. The last one was Julia Farron, long time friend from our company days and a teacher at the school. Alison had tried to have Hanneke Berlage over from Holland but she unfortunately had to cancel at the last moment, but sent a message.

Following this, Tom started to play some of his beautiful music and all the ex-graduates rose from their seats and came down all the aisles to be on stage behind me. What a touching moment! I was then given a most beautiful Tom Merrifield bronze of Dame Alicia Markova, quite exquisite at every turn. A large book was then given to hold all the tributes, cards and photographs and a cheque towards a new garden. These kind gifts were from members of the two Royal Ballet Companies, ex-graduates from the course, and members of the staff from both schools. It was now very moving and hard to keep the tears away, but I was so grateful for all the work that had gone into this special occasion.

To complete this memorable day, a tea party had been arranged, and because the rain had now stopped, a table and two chairs had been placed in the courtyard for my mother and myself under a large sunshade. There we were given tea and cakes. The graduates then queued up to have a few words before leaving. It was wonderful to see so many that I had not seen for years and to be able to thank them personally for coming.

This had been quite a unique occasion in the history of The Royal Ballet School and certainly one I shall never forget. I was so grateful to everyone who had arranged it all and to the many friends and colleagues for being there to share the day with me. To have both Madam and my mother there was wonderful on this most memorable day of my life.

Chapter 15

My return to The Teachers' Training Course

For many years my mother and I had planned to return to Bournemouth and during the summer holiday we once again went to see estate agents in order to get the feel of the market, and see if there was anything available which suited us.

Alison had invited me to teach one day a week, until the time came for us to move. The classes consisted of teaching the ex-professionals and the RAD Solo Seal, both of which I really enjoyed doing. For the rest of my time, I was able to do things that I had never had the opportunity of doing before.

Later in the autumn I received a letter from Lynn Wallis at the RAD, inviting me to conduct the class for the Adeline Genée Awards in January 1996. This is an international competition with candidates entering from all parts of the world.

There would be two classes a day leading up to the 6th of January, which would then be the finalists only for one class. On the 7th of January it would be on stage at Sadler's Wells Theatre for the Finalists' Class Rehearsal in the morning, and warm-up prior to the Adeline Genée Awards in the evening. It was certainly a privilege to be asked to do this, though quite a nerve-racking experience taking the class in front of a full theatre. Judging by the letters I received afterwards, what I gave them to do must have been suitable for the occasion.

For Diploma Day 1996, Alison asked me if I would present the diplomas, which I was very happy to do. There were six graduates from the Three Year Course and three ex-professionals. Also, the 2nd Years were receiving certificates of completion, which made the presentations go on for much longer.

In September, as no progress had been made with our move to Bournemouth, I continued to teach one day a week for the course. There were four ex-professionals that year and it was a pleasure for me to work with them.

During that term, I heard from the Koninklijk Conservatorium, inviting me to the 40th anniversary of when I opened the Ballet School, to be held on 11th January 1997.

(Somehow they had the date wrong, because it should have been the previous September.) However, I was not able to attend, because I was unable to leave my mother at that time. As this was the situation, they asked if I could send a video of a message that they could show on a screen in the theatre. When in The Royal Ballet School, I went to the company office and asked if there was someone who could help me with this, and yes, there was someone who could help me the next day, before he had to go away. Again, how wonderfully the way things do work out. We filmed it in the School library in a very simple way, but it worked and I was able to send it to arrive just in time for their big day. Afterwards I received many messages from former pupils and students, saying how much they had missed me, but that the video had made up for it, as they could actually see me talking.

Ten years later at the 50th anniversary, I was able to attend and see the wonderful building which the Koninklijk Conservatorium now had after having to wait for it so many years. It was certainly a very happy occasion to see so many friends and to be able to stay with my good friend, Hanneke.

For Diploma Day 1997, Alison again asked me if I would present the diplomas, which I was happy to do. There were thirteen graduates from the Three Year Course and four ex-professionals. As in the previous year, there were also the completion certificates to present to the 2nd Years.

It also gave me the opportunity and great pleasure to pay my tribute to Thomas McLelland Young, as he was retiring from The Royal Ballet School that year. I said that it was a great honour for me to be able to thank him and that 'the boot was now on the other foot', as he had spoken at my retirement.

On behalf of the school, I spoke as follows,

'We have been so privileged to have you playing the piano for us for so many years, thirty one in all. I remember watching classes when you were playing for Madam, not always an easy task.

You have been associated with the Teachers' Course since you arrived on the scene and our Friday morning classes were a special feature. Often, past graduates would come back on that day, both to watch the class and listen to your music. While on the course, they had learnt so much from you when you were teaching them in the Music classes.

I know we had a very special musical rapport and something I shall always treasure. You always seemed to know exactly what to play. I only needed to move an arm or leg and you were off, so to speak. I know that between us, we were able to give quite a lot of musical instruction to the classes about blending the music and feeling for movement.

Some years ago, you were kind enough to make tapes for the graduates of piano music for classes, in order to help them, especially if they were unable to have a pianist to play for them. I know that these are being played all over the world. What a wonderful gift for them and how grateful they must be.

You are not only a brilliant pianist and organist but also a composer who has won a number of awards both here and abroad. Dear Tom, we thank you so much from the bottom of our hearts and wish you and your family all the very best.'

In September 1997 I continued as before, teaching one day a week for the course.

At the end of April the following year, after having a holiday in Bournemouth, and so very nearly finding a new home there, our world was suddenly turned upside down. The day after our return to London, I received a telephone call from Dame Merle, asking if I could return to The Royal Ballet School to run the Teachers' Course, as due to unforeseen circumstances, Alison was unable to return after the Easter break. I said I would do it just for one term, thinking of all those sixteen students who would be graduating that year, the largest group I had ever known, plus the two ex-professionals.

The thought of all the examinations to arrange, the reports to write, Diploma Day to sort out and produce a Programme of Dances, was an absolute nightmare. The whole thing seemed an impossibility to achieve in the eight weeks we had left before the end of term. I had not taught these students before, so I did not know them, or they me. What a challenge! Also, I was only on the timetable to teach those graduating once a week, so how would it be possible to make them into a team in that short space of time?

The Head of Education had informed all the parents of the situation and called a meeting for them to meet me, at which he told them that the course was in 'safe hands'.

Since I had left many changes had taken place and it took me some time to really get a clear picture of how things worked. At that time the secretary was also the course co-ordinator and seemed to be running everything, which was a tough job. As Alison was not there to teach the Spanish classes, I called on Sandra Doling, an ex-graduate, to take over the classes.

At the first class I gave, I started to teach them the famous Diploma Day barre, and as the students found it really difficult, I wondered whether I should make changes, but decided I would stick with it and give them the chance to rise to the occasion. The rest of the class for Diploma Day, I arranged as before, with *enchaînements* that I felt would suit them. A few weeks before, I had to ask for more time with them.

The other problem I had to face was not having Tom Young, my pianist friend, who knew all the requirements needed musically for this occasion. Having someone else was certainly not the same and made things much harder for me.

Arranging the Programme of Dances was not easy. The students seemed to have their own ideas of what they would like to show, but they did not understand that they were not all suitable for this occasion. However, in the end we were able to sort out a programme agreeable to all. I must say, I had never faced this problem before!

To cut a long story short, we did make it to Diploma Day with everything completed. How, I will never know! Hope Keelan had to go abroad for a teaching commitment, so I was unable to call on her for any assistance.

On Diploma Day I welcomed everyone, and together with Dame Merle, we presented the diplomas, the awards and certificates of completion for the 2nd Years. Dame Merle read out a letter from Alison to the graduates. She also wanted us to give a new award to two of the graduates for 'An outstanding contribution to the Theatre Course'.

At the end of July the course co-ordinator left the job because she was exhausted and needed a rest.

Dame Merle had been due to retire at the end of July but agreed to stay on for a further term, until Gailene Stock, the new director, would arrive from Australia in the new year. So it was Dame Merle and the Head of Education who asked me if I could continue until the half-term in October. I said I could only accept if I had my former assistant, Hope Keelan, to help me, because we had worked together so successfully in the past. I also knew that I could not give as much time to the course as I had done in the past when I was director.

Hope was at that time freelancing in London, but agreed to help as much as possible around the work she already had. She would be made the course co-ordinator and I accepted the position of part-time Principal.

As the Governors had the previous year decided to close the course in 2000 there were now only two groups, the 2nd and 3rd Years, to deal with. Also, no ex-professionals had been accepted onto the course, so the whole thing would be easier to manage.

In September 1998 it was certainly good to be working with Hope again and I re-arranged the timetable to fit the situation. We were then able to go ahead.

By October there was still no news from Alison and I was asked to continue until Christmas. By now, I was feeling that this was going on longer than I really wanted and I felt it was not fair to my mother, who was really wanting to move out of London.

In December we had the usual 'In House Day', for parents and friends. This time we invited the former dancing teachers of the students to attend. As in past years I gave a classical class to the 2nd and 3rd Years, and this was followed by some dances.

In January I was asked if I could continue until July 2000 when the course was closing, as Alison would not be returning. There was really no choice because I did not want to cause any more disruption to the students, and I also wanted it to finish on the high standard that had been set before. I think my mother could understand my reasoning.

That month we welcomed Gailene Stock as the new Director of The Royal Ballet School.

From then on, Hope and I just pressed forward with our programme of work and the students were settled and working well for us.

Diploma Day had arrived once again, after a much easier preparation than the year before. There were only six graduates, so

I had been able to give them more of my time helping them in class.

We were as usual in the Arnold Haskell Theatre Studio, showing the Demonstration Class and Programme of Dances and this year I had another pianist.

At the presentation time, I welcomed everyone and especially Gailene Stock, as it was her first time with us on this occasion. Hope read out the names and Gailene presented the diplomas, and I gave my usual speech. This was all followed by the reception in the Sadler's Wells Studio.

My mother had not been finding things too easy for a while and at the end of July it became necessary for her to have more care than I could give her. I was able to arrange for her to go to a care home in Kent, where I knew she would have all the loving care she needed. I went to visit the first time by train and then Hope kindly took me by car, to show me how easy it was for me to drive there. I can never thank her enough for that, because it made it possible for me to visit and even stay there for days at a time.

Come September 1999 I knew I was on the last lap, with just one more year to go. I was so grateful to have such a hard working and co-operative group of students to work with, and they certainly completed the course at the high standard which we had worked to achieve over the years. There were nine of them, including one boy, Gustavo Quintins, who had been awarded the Cyril Beaumont Scholarship for his last year of study. Without financial help, he would have been unable to stay and complete the course. He was a very deserving case, and this was proved when he gained the highest examination results and other awards on Diploma Day.

In the middle of January 2000, I suddenly felt that it was time that I brought my mother home. With the help of visiting nurses I was able to manage, and it was lovely to have her with me again.

The 'In House Day' was held in February, later than usual, but I gave the classical class and we followed this with some dances. The parents, friends and the students' former dancing teachers all seemed to enjoy the afternoon and I was able to talk to the parents.

As this was to be the last Diploma Day for the Teachers' Course, it was decided to once again hold the celebrations at White Lodge, as when I retired the first time in 1995, since more people were expected to attend.

On Sunday the 16th of July, invited guests, parents, ex-graduates and many friends gathered in the Margot Fonteyn Theatre in Richmond Park, and I was so happy that with the help of a very good friend, my mother was able to be there too. Tom Young my wonderful pianist, was also there, although he too had to be helped, as he was now in a wheelchair.

John Mitchell, the Academic Principal at White Lodge, said in welcoming the capacity audience: 'Miss Adams IS the Teachers' Course' and quoting Morecombe and Wise, quipped, 'You can't see the join.' All that was quite moving and at that moment, I really was grateful to have seen the course come full circle. I did say it felt rather strange to be standing there once more, after receiving such a wonderful send off when I retired the first time.

We started as usual with the Diploma Day barre, which the graduates had perfected to a very high standard, and the rest of the class went well. This was soon followed by the Programme of Dances. There were twelve items, which included the Morning Hours from *Coppélia*; the Blue Boy from *Les Patineurs*; as a tribute to Madam, the Betrayed Girl from *Rake's Progress*; the *Peasant Pas de Deux* from *Giselle*, including the two solos and finale; the Black Queen and Red Knight from *Checkmate*, another tribute for Madam; plus two Spanish dances, the *Farouka* and the *Sevillianas*. Lisa, being Scottish, showed a traditional dance, and the programme finished with a contemporary number choreographed by Ross McKim to Tom Young's composition, danced as a tribute to Tom.

During the gaps between items eleven and twelve, I gave an account of how the Teachers' Course was started and all the teachers who had been involved over the years. As Mary Goodhew said in her article in the *Dancing Times*, 'Quite a Who's Who of Ballet!' I also read the original advertisement which was placed in the *Dancing Times* in 1964.

After a short break the graduates were then ready for the presentations. Gailene Stock was at the table with Hope. I welcomed everyone and said that I had received a letter from Madam sending her good wishes to all and looking forward to hearing all about the day from her secretary, Mrs Quinelle, who was there with her husband.

We then proceeded with presenting the diplomas and awards. In her speech, Gailene said 'how important teachers are in inspiring and motivating the stars of tomorrow'. She hoped that 'all the 324

graduates in 26 countries would keep in touch with the school.'
This reminded me of the first time that Madam presented the
diplomas and said 'that her gift to them was to allow them to watch
classes at the school.' This was followed by the head student. I then
'congratulated the graduates on their successful completion of the
course – the examination results had been very good and what we
would expect from a group who had worked so hard and had a
tremendous team spirit. They were now going out as Ambassadors
for The Royal Ballet School, to join the others around the world.'

I then thanked all the teachers and pianists who had contributed
so much to the success of the course. Then my special thanks to
Vivienne Saxton and Denise Winmill, who had helped so much
with the course over the years. Last but not least, my gratitude to
Hope, without whose help none of this would have been possible.
It was truly amazing what she had been able to accomplish in the
last few weeks leading up to this day, after having an operation on
her foot and staggering around on crutches. All the arrangements
concerning that day and running through my prepared class under
those circumstances was nothing less than miraculous. I was so glad
to hear later that Gailene had offered her the position of Assistant
Ballet Principal at White Lodge.

I then announced that a 'Teachers' Course Association' had been
started, and that we would meet at White Lodge each year. I hoped
that as many as possible would become members. I ended by saying
that I thought that 'Madam's dream had been honoured'. The day
finished with a lovely reception in the salon, and as it was a beautiful
day, everyone was able to go out into the gardens.

To close, Madam passed on in 2001, and my mother in 2002. I
happily returned to Bournemouth near the sea six months later, to
a bungalow which found me, so to speak, after all that looking my
mother and I had done those years before.

I am now able to enjoy my freedom, after giving fifty years to
The Royal Ballet organisation. However, I have been invited to the
school performance each year, which has been a treat, and I make
a regular visit to White Lodge for the Teachers' Course Association
Day. It is so lovely to see the many happy faces after they have been
allowed to watch the classes there in the morning. Then we have
lunch together and are able to have a chat. After that, there is the
'de Valois Junior Choreographic Competition', which is always so

interesting to see, and I am sure must give the graduates some fresh ideas.

Then several awards are given, mine included. This latter award is given to the student who has shown exceptional 'Dance Quality and Musicality'. The student is chosen by members of the Ballet Staff. The name of this mark of recognition is:

'The Valerie Adams Award.'

'In gratitude to 'Madam' for forming the Teachers' Course'.

I do hope that over the years I have been able to share that love of dance and the beauty of movement blending with the music which so inspired me to want to dance. I have always felt such joy and enthusiasm when teaching, and hope that this has in some way radiated to all with whom I have been in contact. To be able to see improvement going on in front of ones eyes when giving a correction, is one of the most satisfying and wonderful things to behold.

1995. Together with 'Madam'. Photo: Mike Martin.

Appendix

A few little gems from 'Madam's' teaching

The following statements are all things which Madam insisted upon when she was teaching and I include them here, hoping that they may be of help to those who are interested.

She always said that the exercises at the barre were a preparation for the ones in the centre. In other words, like tuning an instrument before playing a wonderful piece. The ones mentioned below are in no particular order.

She insisted on correct placement and that the weight is evenly distributed either between both legs or on the supporting leg.

At the barre when preparing for an exercise, from the moment one begins to move ones hands, the eyes must take the movement, never the hands and then the eyes.

Pliés. Timing should be even, the same coming up as going down, with well co-ordinated *ports de bras*. Making sure the hips are level and the weight is evenly distributed. With a feeling of going up as you go down, and using your legs to come up, and a good feeling of lift at the end.

When including a circular *ports de bras*, as you recover from the forward bend, let the hand lift the body into a true side bend with arm over your head. Not one that has already started to go into the back bend. This was something that Madam used to get very cross about, if the hips and shoulders started to turn when they should stay facing the front.

Any time that one had a rise, whether on two feet or one, the whole body had to stretch and lift up from the feet right through to the top of the head and beyond, and that feeling had to come through the face, cheek bones and eyelashes.

Battements tendus. The toes must never leave the floor. Have a full length of the leg without distorting the hips, especially in 2nd position, where the temptation is to allow the weight to shift off the supporting leg. The body must always lift before releasing the leg. She was not keen on a very slow release, she wanted the movement to go through the foot but to go out to the extension quite quickly and then return to 5th with the weight placed firmly on the floor

Battements glissés. Keep the toes pointing down closely to the floor, not more than 5 cms. The movement should be quick and sharp with a stop at the end of each extension. She wanted good use of the ankle joint. This being a preparation for *échappé relevés* and *sautés* and all quick *terre à terre* work.

Ronds de jambe à terre. As in *battements tendus,* make full use of the half way position between front and side and side and back without pulling off the supporting leg. Making sure also that the working foot comes straight through the 1st position and not over crossing the heel of the supporting foot. She would stand in front of the student and place her foot in line with the heel of the supporting foot so that they could not cross over and say 'don't touch me'. That was sure to make them do it right.

Battements frappés sur le cou-de-pied. Again these should be sharp with toes pointing down towards the floor and a hold at the end of each extension. The thigh held absolutely still, as the movement comes only from the knee down.

Battements fondus. Make sure the hips are level and that the supporting leg is going down straight. Again with the feeling of going up as you go down. She made you have an accurate understanding of where to open the leg at 45% and at 90%.

Ronds de jambe en l'air. Madam always said if done correctly, this was a very strengthening exercise for the knee joint. She insisted that whatever level the leg was raised to, be it base of the calf, knee height or higher, then the toe comes in to make a circle in front, and extending at exactly the same height. There must be no lifting of the thigh on the extension. The same applied to both *en dehors* and *en dedans.*

Grands battements. Before releasing the leg there must be a lift of the body, and again when the leg comes down on the slight hesitation, before closing. Going to the 2nd position, hips must be square to the front and weight on the supporting leg. During the barre exercises, Madam was often saying 'hand off the barre' to check that the student was on balance.

Adage. Madam always made sure that the students understood the track that the toe was making when it left the floor, and after reaching *retiré,* the knee must lift before opening out into the position. Once there it must be held in position.

Grands battements en cloche. She insisted on the use of the floor when passing through the 1st position. This she said was preparing for *grands jetés en tournant* and *grands fouettés sautés* and all those types of movement. How important it was to lift the body before lifting the leg to the front and how helpful it was when jumping. At the end of this exercise, it was quite usual to hear Madam say 'hand off'. It was not a time to get the balance but to be already on it, so it had to come off in rhythm at the end of the exercise.

In the centre, with *Ports de Bras* there had to be a lift of the body before moving the arms. The arms had to be always kept within the frame work – if the arms were in 2nd position, one should be able to look straight forward and just see the tips of the fingers out of the corner of the eyes. They should never be behind the shoulders, unless it was in the ballet *Swan Lake.* Then she said it was the characterisation of a swan. Madam would often say, 'you have a back', use it. She meant that when the arms were at the side, you must feel the stretch across the back. She said it was the sides of the body which supported the arms, under the elbow and wrist. The muscles then, between the shoulder and the elbow, and the elbow and the wrist must be relaxed and the fingers kept easy with no strain whatsoever.

In a lecture Madam once gave to the school, she talked about 'projection' and said how important it was for students to understand. She then proceeded to tell everyone to sit up straight, and to look out and really send their vision forward. Then she said look back inside your head and out at the back. Then she said look forward again, and after repeating it several more times, said, that was true 'projection.' I always remember as a student in the school always being told to project by both Madam and Ailne Phillips. Madam often remarked how well the Turkish dancers used their eyes.

When the arms were in 3rd position, one in the front and the other at the side, preparing for a *pirouette,* that is when she would be insisting that the student had square placement with the arms. If it was a *relevé* preparation, that they did not climb up, but do a strong *relevé,* holding the foot under the knee, and then put the foot down quickly with quick pressure into the floor for the *pirouette.* She always said the floor was there to help you. Still on *pirouettes* she insisted on a very fast use of the head, and said 'you must spot with your eyes, I only want to see your face'. Many a time have I seen her stand in front of the student with her finger up in front of their eyes, making them use their head faster.

Madam would say that the centre practice needed all the demands of the exercises at the barre and more, and would on occasions take the students straight into the centre leaving out the barre work altogether. *Jetés battements, petite battements sautés, flic flac* and *ronds de jambe sautés*, one or more were always included in this section.

With *Adage* she would insist on the full use of dynamics, what went up, had to go up and the same with down and also if it had to go to the side. She always wanted the student to be in the position in good time to be able to hold it and gain strength. The focus of the eyes was also important because that gives balance. In an *arabesque* she always wanted you to feel beyond the end of the fingers. She said you must reach up and beyond and then relax in a position, but not collapse! The *adage* exercises she gave, were always quite straightforward and not long, but always very demanding.

Allegro steps were often very tricky, moving in a way you did not really expect. She would often set the steps first and make the students keep their arms down in *bras bas*. Then she would arrange a different arm movement for each step, which was often a nightmare to be able to make it in the right place on time. The other thing she was famous for, was suddenly in the middle of an exercise, calling out 'reverse it'. Which meant, that if the exercise was going forward, without stopping it now had to be repeated going backwards, this also applied to *petite batterie* exercises.

Petite batterie, had to be kept close to the floor, hardly jumping at all. If a student was jumping too high, she would walk across and place her hand on their head to stop them from going up. She said, that keeping down made the students use their feet and legs quicker and produced sharper beats. She again insisted that the arms be kept in *bras bas* (very Irish) so that all the concentration was in the feet.

The other thing she liked to do towards the end of a class, was to start off with the third exercise she had given, then go to the first and perhaps the fourth and then the second jumbling them all up. She always seemed to remember what they were, even if the students did not.

With *Grands allegro* she was insistent on the full use of dynamics of movement, as mentioned before under *adage*. She really would make her students travel by putting herself in the position on the floor where she wanted them to be. The floor pattern and design were very important to her and were all part of the whole.

After the *grands allegro* steps, Madam often finished her classes with a quick turning step coming *en diagonal* from the corner and it was done at great speed, with sharp use of the head. This of course being before the usual *changements* and *grands battements* to finish, which she always did.

There was never any time wasted when Madam was teaching, the students were kept on the go all the time, even if she did want to repeat exercises until she was completely satisfied that they understood what she wanted.

Madam always said 'technique without the feeling for movement and dance was no good, technique is only a means to an end, you must share it with the audience.' She said that an *enchaînement* or a dance should be like a painting, full of colour and movement.

Madam shared with me many little gems, and oh, how grateful I was to have had that privilege of working so closely with her. Lastly she said, 'your students should leave your class better than when they went in'. That is what I feel teaching is all about!

The Royal Ballet School Teachers' Course
Diploma Graduates 1966 - 2000

1966
Hilary Bingley
Catherine Haggarty
Valerie Hunt
Elizabeth Hurst
Jean Pestereff
Ruth Silk
Anne Wheatley
1967
Annik Coatalen
Beverley-Ann Moore
Tania Tang
1968
Alison Bailey
Athene Blackwood (deceased)
Catherine Wendy Jones
Pauline King
Jane Robinson
1969
Heather Fish
Valerie Haigh
Gay Harrison
Zoe Horn
Tukta Jalavicherana
Evelyn Johnson (deceased)
Sylvia McCully
Rosemary Pigot
Deborah Sims
Susan Smith
Maria Tsarouchis
1970
Jemima Bannerman
Susi Della-Pietra
Kate Flatt
Astrid Hayward
Carol Haws-Jones

1970 cont.
Shirley Lucking
Deirdre Watts
1971
Judith Hoare
Susan King
Jane Slocombe
1972
Louise Bennett
Susan Downer
Monica Gallagher
Janina Gieralt
Lucy Harrison
Naomi Long
Deborah Phillips
Sheila Roper
Christine Sparkes
Susan Spencer
Elizabeth Varrall
Tina Young
1973
Tandy Hiranyasthiti
Patrica Prince
Elizabeth Rae
Cheryll Roddick
Christine Stevens
Jane Wilson
1974
Catherine Allan
Briget Allen
Hilary Craig
Janet Cross
Teresa Mann
Carol Mole
Gail Woodward

1975
Priscilla Bell
Diana Choy
Lisa Fusillo
Katie Gunn
Sylvia Hubbard
Wendy Lewis
Caroline Pavely
Susan Wells
1976
Sarah Bullitt
Helen Coope
Karen Hale
Hope Keelan
Karen Large
Gillian Perry
Christine Reynolds
Joanne Woodcock
1977
Sally Baker
Rosemary Denny
Susan Durant
Jennifer Hockaday
Virginia Markwick
Deborah Morgan
Vivienne Saxton
Julia Stevens
1978
Louisa McAlpine
Debbie McGee
Anthony Armstrong-Jones
1979
Melanie Agar
Nuchavadi Bamrungtrakun
Amanda Buxton
Diane Durant
Tania Fairbairn
Susan Glasser
Leonora Gregory
Hélène Iseli
Terance James
Caroline Jenkins

1979 cont.
Elizabeth Mills
Deborah Prior
Fiona Grantham Smith
Alexandra Young
1980
Sandra Doling
Kathryn Holmes
Gillian Hurst
Nicola Lawson (deceased)
Lorna Martin
Vararom Pachimsawat
Lesley Richardson
Petra Taylor
1981
Louise Cheyne
Barbara MacGregor
Laura Madden
Donald McLennan
Anne Romyn
Denise Winmill
1982
Helen Daniels
Guy Davies
Michele Endley
Annette Fitzgerald
Nicola Hayes
Sandra Hyams
Ann Jarvis
Yupin Lee
Jessica Shenton
Wendy Smale
Penny Withers
Dudley von Loggenburg TCPD
1983
Cheryl Doyle
Susan Hawksley
Alison Hayward
Victoria Lowin
Joanne Lundy
Melisa Mackie
Janet Markowski (Zoe Austin)

1983 cont.

Tracey Warner
Sylvia Yong
Sheelagh Lonergan TCPD

1984

Amanda Davies
Wendy Griffin
Marian Hayward
Seong Yoko Ho
Anna Lantz
Carolyn Neesham
Sally Prout
Linda Virgoe
David Picken TCPD

1985

Helen Farrell
Fiona Hayward
Jeanette Hull
Alexandra Irwin
Joanne McKears
Clare Merchant
Samantha Mose (deceased)
Sally Webster
Joanne Wesley
Linden Currey TCPD
Susanne Lindstrom TCPD
Ludmilla Molenaar TCPD

1986

Jayne Cooper
Julie Cronshaw
Julia Ellis
Nichole Fitzpatrick
Sarah Hanson
Hsien Sheng Ho
Sally Hodder
Sally Horsley
Juliette MacKenzie
Paloma Peterson
Joanne Redfearn
Hariklia Theotokatos

1987

Tanya Herbert
Alison Maidment
Cordelia O'Neill
Claire Rowland
Sian Sullivan
Amanda Maxwell TCPD
Jill Porter TCPD
Ruth Prior TCPD

1988

Caroline Barrett
Sarah Boocock
Mee Lin Fong
Kew Yoke Ho
Brona MacNally
Nuria Martinez
Elizabeth McCarthy
Sally-Anne Naunton
Jane Pratt
Anthony Sewell TCPD

1989

Rosemary Cokayne
Sarah-Ann Dicker
China Hiruta
Zara Hodgkinson
Susanne Jones
Dimitra Kouremeti
Mondakhan Pramoj
Nicola Regan

1990

Elspeth Daly
Valerie Forsyth
Wendy Holt
Clare Howarth
Nicola Kennedy
Sara Knight
Lisa Rager
Deborah Smith
Mary Goodhew TCPD
Vittoria Minucci TCPD
Frances White TCPD

1991
Melanie Baird
Julie Fleming
Emma Gannon
Emma Teresa Hallam
Anna Meadmore
Joanna Pegler
Helen Taylor
Yasmin Taylor
Caroline Jennings TCPD
Long Ong TCPD
Aydin Ord TCPD
1992
Mariella Archontides
Tina Chen
Beverley-Ann Drew
Nicola Grant
Fleur Jones
Heidi Kimber
Natalie Pollard
Nicola Roberts
Li Lin Wong
Veronique Beliot TCPD
Miki Norii TCPD
1993
Danella Bedford
Lucy Clay
Lyn Fitzsimons
Yasuko Goro
Anwin Mannings
Lowri Mannings
Kyoko Matsumoto
Audrey McKerron
Sonja Tinnes
Natalie Wraight
Kate Wray
Anna Chan TCPD
Ikuko Hirano TCPD

1994
Emma Brawn
Carol Clarke
Linzi Else
Dawn Foley
Nicola Heaton
Penny Kay
Rosalind Sacre
Hannah Simpson
Graham Fletcher TCPD
Li Jiong TCPD
Hiroko Nishikawa TCPD
Kafuyu Shintani TCPD
1995
Charlotte Anderson
Danielle Bond
Emily Borthwick
Rosemary MacGregor
Philip Pegler
Alexandra Sherman
Emma Spears
Katherine Wood
James Supervia TCPD
1996
Anna Atkinson
Catherine Gill
Carolyn Ross
Mikah Smillie
Laura Snowball
Elisa Tang
Hany Abdin TCPD
Lai Sheung Chan TCPD
So Hon Wah TCPD
Stephan Xavier TCPD
1997
Joanne Bennett
Natasha Carson
Victoria Collinson
Lisa Davies
Judith Harris
Lisa Haynes
Bethan Mogford

1997 cont:-
Sonya Nichols
Joanne Russell
Liz Stride
Katie Stringer
Maria Vasilou
Suzanne Yong
Hedda Cooke TCPD
Yukie Fujino TCPD
Ravenna Tucker TCPD
David Yow TCPD
1998
Hayley Allen
Anna Berryman
Nicky Bitsaktsi
Greet Boterman
Helen Bray
Susanne Buckle
Holly Coombes
Hazel Gold
Rebecca Jackson
Kristina Johannessen-Conders
Verity Mason
Tara Rogutski
Jennifer Schwartz
Louise Shaw
Lucie Weaver
Jessica Williams
Jeremy Allen TCPD
Yuko Hirayama TCPD
1999
Josephine Darvill-Mills
Anna Hunter
Na Ye Kim
Victoria Maitland
Tamsin Putman
Effie Sotira

2000
Victoria Anderson
Gustavo Beserra-Quintans
Carmen Duncan
Katie Gilkerson
Vanessa Gould
Leanne McIndoe
Sarah Moulson
Lisa Ritchie
Laura Willis

Acknowledgements

I am deeply grateful for the spiritual inspiration and support I have received from the study of Christian Science throughout my life.

I would like to thank my two dear friends Shirley Reid and Ray Seddon for kindly reading through my draft and giving me such helpful suggestions.

Towards the completion of his task, for which I am most grateful, Ray wrote the following verse, which I think makes a fitting ending to my story.

THE BALLET

The grace and rhythm of the dance
Unite with music to enhance
The wealth of beauty in each heart,
Fresh joy, new vision, to impart;
In such delights, our days rehearse
The rhythms of the universe.

Lightning Source UK Ltd.
Milton Keynes UK
UKOW03n2247270214

227282UK00002B/8/P